# The Foreign Service and American Public Opinion

Dynamics and Prospects

MICHAEL S. POLLARD, CHARLES P. RIES, SOHAELA AMIRI

Sponsored by the Una Chapman Cox Foundation

For more information on this publication, visit www.rand.org/t/RRA1845-1.

### About RAND

The RAND Corporation is a research organization that develops solutions to public policy challenges to help make communities throughout the world safer and more secure, healthier and more prosperous. RAND is nonprofit, nonpartisan, and committed to the public interest. To learn more about RAND, visit www.rand.org.

### Research Integrity

Our mission to help improve policy and decisionmaking through research and analysis is enabled through our core values of quality and objectivity and our unwavering commitment to the highest level of integrity and ethical behavior. To help ensure our research and analysis are rigorous, objective, and nonpartisan, we subject our research publications to a robust and exacting quality-assurance process; avoid both the appearance and reality of financial and other conflicts of interest through staff training, project screening, and a policy of mandatory disclosure; and pursue transparency in our research engagements through our commitment to the open publication of our research findings and recommendations, disclosure of the source of funding of published research, and policies to ensure intellectual independence. For more information, visit www.rand.org/about/principles.

RAND's publications do not necessarily reflect the opinions of its research clients and sponsors.

Published by the RAND Corporation, Santa Monica, Calif.
© 2022 RAND Corporation
RAND® is a registered trademark.

Library of Congress Cataloging-in-Publication Data is available for this publication.
ISBN: 978-1-9774-0900-3

*Cover image: bluraz/Adobe Stock.*

### Limited Print and Electronic Distribution Rights

This publication and trademark(s) contained herein are protected by law. This representation of RAND intellectual property is provided for noncommercial use only. Unauthorized posting of this publication online is prohibited; linking directly to its webpage on rand.org is encouraged. Permission is required from RAND to reproduce, or reuse in another form, any of its research products for commercial purposes. For information on reprint and reuse permissions, please visit www.rand.org/pubs/permissions.

# About This Report

With the support of the Una Chapman Cox Foundation, the RAND Corporation has undertaken an in-depth, nonpartisan, and empirical examination of American public opinion related to diplomacy, diplomats, and the Foreign Service, with the goal of illuminating the dynamics that affect them.

In May 2020, we fielded a series of questions probing attitudes about recruitment, priorities, and challenges affecting American diplomats to a nationally representative probability-based sample of 2,026 Americans age 24 and older. Respondents were participants in RAND's American Life Panel (ALP).

Based on results of the panel, RAND staff recruited and moderated in-depth online focus groups around the country.[1] Focus group discussions were led by RAND researchers and designed to tease out finer insights on public attitudes and probe their dynamics (e.g., how opinions about diplomacy are formed; attitudes about risks, alliance-tending, consular services, business support, and the many other aspects of Foreign Service work).

In the first half of 2021, the questions from the 2020 survey were asked again of the same ALP participants, with several additional questions that emerged from the focus group discussions. The second survey enabled examination of changes in attitudes between the two years and the factors associated with those changes.

This report begins with a summary of previous public opinion polling on American diplomacy, presents the findings of the two ALP surveys and the focus group discussions, and concludes with a distillation of key findings and policy implications. It probes public opinion regarding diplomacy, its purposes, and its practitioners, as well as what the evidence suggests are ways to increase public understanding and engagement about diplomacy and the work of Foreign Service Officers.

## National Security Research Division

This research was supported by the Una Chapman Cox Foundation and conducted within the International Security and Defense Policy Center of the RAND National Security Research Division (NSRD). NSRD conducts research and analysis for the Office of the Secretary of Defense, the U.S. Intelligence Community, the U.S. State Department, allied foreign governments, and foundations.

For more information on the RAND International Security and Defense Policy Center, see www.rand.org/nsrd/isdp or contact the director (contact information is provided on the webpage).

---

[1] Focus groups were conducted virtually because of the ongoing coronavirus pandemic.

## Acknowledgments

The authors would like to thank the trustees of the Una Chapman Cox Foundation for their vision and steadfast support for this project. We thank Cathy Novelli, president of Listening for America, for her ideas and insights that helped us craft our focus group topics. We also thank David Grant, Karen Edwards, and Julie Newell for their assistance in programming and implementing the ALP surveys and Melissa Bradley and Danielle Schlang for their skill in developing and facilitating the focus groups. Monique Martineau provided valuable assistance as we prepared the final document.

As part of RAND's quality assurance process, this report had two reviewers, one a RAND colleague (Marek Posard) and one an external expert, Ambassador (Ret.) E. Anthony Wayne. The authors are grateful for their helpful feedback. Agnes Schaefer and King Mallory provided comments throughout the project that allowed us to improve the final document. Any errors are the authors' own.

# Summary

American public opinion on international affairs has been well studied. For 45 years, the Chicago Council on Global Affairs (CCGA) has conducted an annual survey of attitudes toward U.S. engagement with international partners and adversaries. Similarly, Pew Research Center has surveyed American opinion on global challenges, and it has asked the same questions in many other countries around the world. These surveys well document the pulse of American attitudes about international affairs and our place in the world.

But what do Americans think about those who conduct U.S. diplomacy, the members of the U.S. Foreign Service, and other American officials who represent the nation abroad, help citizens in trouble, and seek to advance American interests in a changing world? This report is aimed at understanding current attitudes about the men and women engaged in diplomacy in the Foreign Service and ascertaining the reasons for such attitudes. The authors suggest implications of our findings for the State Department, the present and future administrations, members of Congress, and others interested in increasing understanding and support around the country for diplomacy.

## Research Approach

In May 2020, we fielded a series of questions probing attitudes about recruitment, priorities, and challenges affecting American diplomats to a nationally representative probability-based sample of 2,026 Americans age 24 and over. Respondents were participants in RAND's American Life Panel (ALP). In June 2021, we re-surveyed 1,829 of the same panel participants asking the same questions, buttressed in some cases by wording modifications that arose in our analysis of the first survey.

Between the two ALP surveys, RAND researchers led 14 focus groups across the country to probe 118 representative Americans further on the reasons for their views on American diplomacy and diplomats that emerged in the nationwide survey. Recruited members of the groups were not taken from the ALP and were balanced by gender, demographic category, education, and region. Though intended to be conducted in person, the focus groups took place virtually because of the coronavirus pandemic, and group members were offered technical support with installing and operating the required video meeting software[2] to reduce bias in the sample.

Our 2020 and 2021 ALP questionnaires and the protocol that our moderators used for the focus groups are in Appendix A, B, and D, respectively. Appendix C presents the details of a selection of key statistical analyses.

---

[2] Participants had to already have a way to access the internet—either computer, tablet, or phone.

## Key Findings

Below are our key findings from the ALP surveys and 14 focus groups, presented by topic.
- **Impressions of diplomacy and American diplomats** were generally favorable.
  - Favorable attitudes were stable between 2020 and 2021, with 37 percent of survey respondents having a favorable or very favorable view of American diplomats in 2021, against only 5 percent with an unfavorable or very unfavorable opinion. The "no opinion" response was significant as well, at 25 percent. Respondents with greater knowledge of the Foreign Service reported more-favorable views. Those with less knowledge were also more likely to reply "no opinion" on subsequent questions.
  - During focus groups, many participants admitted that they knew relatively little about the activities and contributions of American diplomats abroad. A few considered that to be a plus: "If you don't hear about it, it must be going well."
- Of the major **functions of diplomats** that were presented, survey and focus group participants were most aware of "helping citizens abroad."
  - Focus group participants also cited "report on developments" abroad and "advance American interests" as important functions, while survey respondents rated "advance U.S. interests with foreign governments" as the second most important function.
  - Survey respondents and focus group participants were not very aware that American diplomats had any engagement with export promotion or business protection.
  - Focus group participants expressed mixed views about "promoting American values" as a function. Some focus group participants considered "values" to be a "loaded term," or divisive in a domestic political context. An additional question regarding values promotion on the 2021 ALP survey provided examples of the specific values promoted, which resulted in a majority support of this function.
- We probed **differences** in favorability toward diplomats and importance of their functions **by demographic characteristics and political views** using the survey data.
  - Men were significantly more likely to have a favorable or very favorable opinion of diplomats than women. Women were more likely to indicate "no opinion."
  - Respondents with higher incomes or higher educational attainments, as well as those who reported voting in 2016, were more likely to view American diplomats favorably. However, political views along a continuum from very liberal to very conservative were not significantly correlated with overall perceptions of favorability.
  - Older respondents were more likely to consider "advancing interests" and "promoting values" to be important, while younger respondents considered "negotiating" more important.
  - Among those with higher incomes and educational attainment, "advancing interests," "promoting values," and "negotiating" were relatively more important, suggesting support for more-proactive functions.

- Those with lower educational attainment and lower incomes prioritized "helping sell products," "determining visas," and "fighting crime and terrorism," emphasizing greater support for *defensive or protective* functions.
- Survey respondents identified "understanding of global affairs" and "negotiating skill" as the **most important skills for diplomats**.
  - "Public speaking," "bravery," "discipline in following instructions," and "empathy" were clustered at the low end of importance.
  - Focus groups provided more-nuanced discussion of skills. Language fluency was often cited as important and related to success in negotiating.
- Most survey respondents (61 percent in 2020 and 55 percent in 2021) had "no opinion" on whether they considered American diplomats to be **representative of American society**.
  - Of those with opinions, in 2020 a slight majority considered diplomats to be representative of American society. This changed in 2021, with a statistically significant 8 percent increase (and a majority) of those indicating that diplomats were *not* representative.
  - Some in focus groups suggested that diversity should not be a selection criterion for diplomats; they should be chosen on the basis of exam scores alone. However, more participants saw the value of a diverse Foreign Service that would be more culturally sensitive and aware and also would "look more like America."
- Focus group participants organically raised the issue of feeling less positively about the **effectiveness of political appointees versus career diplomats**.
  - Participants felt that political appointees were less qualified, less dedicated, and less likely to be working in the public interest, among other opinions.
  - To evaluate these concerns, we added a question to the 2021 ALP survey. It gave background on appointment process and noted that both types of ambassadors are charged with representing administration policies. ALP respondents consistently considered career ambassadors more effective than political ambassadors.
- About half of survey respondents had "no opinion" on whether they considered American diplomats to be **trustworthy or politically biased**.
  - Among those with opinions, the majority considered diplomats to be both trustworthy *and* politically biased. The results were similar in 2020 and 2021.
  - Examples of assumed trustworthiness emerged in the focus groups, but discussions did not surface examples of purported political bias.
- A strong and consistent majority in the ALP surveys (over 65 percent) thought that **diplomacy contributes to national security**.
  - Focus group participants thought that diplomacy allows the nation to negotiate the complexity and volatility of today's world to avoid armed conflicts and solve global problems together with other countries; climate change and pandemics were mentioned a number of times.

- Likewise, more than 40 percent of survey respondents in both years said that it was **better for diplomats to lead efforts abroad than the military**.
  - Focus group participants saw Foreign Services as a way to "promote peace" and thought that other countries would view the military as "aggressive." However, some suggested that the country should rely on the military, not diplomats, to deal with certain threats, such as the Islamic State of Iraq and Syria.
  - Focus group participants did not have fixed views on which parts of the U.S. government should lead foreign policy.
- When asked whether **spending on foreign affairs** should be more, less, or about the same, survey respondents indicated a preference for keeping spending about the same, with relatively more support for cutting than adding to funding in 2020.
  - Our findings were consistent with CCGA and Pew Research Center results for similarly worded questions in previous years.
  - Focus group participants varied in their opinions, though it emerged that most had no point of reference for how much funding the State Department currently receives.
  - Therefore, for the 2021 ALP survey, we modified the spending question for half the sample to provide more context about the amount of the federal budget (1.2 percent to 1.5 percent) that goes to the State Department. In contrast with when respondents did not receive the additional information, we found statistically significant increases in support for increased funding. Even in this case, however, nearly half of the respondents favored keeping funding the same.

## Implications

- Our study documented generally favorable public opinion attitudes toward American diplomats but also found limited understanding of what diplomats actually do, how they are selected, and how diplomacy interacts with other elements of America's national security establishment. More understanding of the critical functions of the Foreign Service among the American public is needed.
- Survey respondents and focus group participants considered support for American citizens abroad to be a core—and much valued—function for diplomats, suggesting that further improving services to American citizens traveling abroad would pay considerable dividends to the State Department and the traveling public.
- Our survey respondents and focus group participants were less aware that diplomats abroad have export promotion and business support responsibilities. Embassies and the State Department may need to be much more deliberate and more public about the support and advocacy they provide to businesses and farmers. Ambassadors should visit American-owned or associated facilities and seek opportunities to articulate the advantages of American companies. Likewise, State Department economic officers should use social media and be ready to take part in domestic business and labor conferences to explain opportunities abroad.

- Among functions carried out by diplomats, survey respondents and focus group participants had mixed views about how much importance they placed on promoting American "values" abroad. When ALP respondents were provided more context for what was meant by values ("democracy, freedom, human rights, and the rule of law") in the second ALP survey, support rose substantially for this function. This suggests that American officials should be explicit with domestic audiences about the values that the Foreign Service promotes abroad and why.
- We found rising concern about whether the Foreign Service was representative of American society. The Secretary of State recently appointed the State Department's first-ever chief diversity and inclusion officer, as part of a broader effort to promote broad representation at all levels of the State Department.[3] Our findings suggest that the State Department should continue to make vigorous and public efforts to improve representation among the ranks of its diplomats.
- Similarly, we found worrisome levels of opinion that American diplomats, while trustworthy, were politically biased. This suggests that the State Department should undertake a dedicated effort to reinforce nonpartisanship among its officials. Our finding that the American public had greater confidence in career ambassadors than political appointees also implies that the public would support reduced politicization of State Department positions.
- When it became clear that more context was needed, we conducted an experiment on a question about level of support for funding foreign affairs by adding a sentence describing State Department funding relative to other federal departments. This yielded a statistically significant increase in support for additional funding when compared with a control group of respondents who did not receive that information. This suggests that efforts to inform the public on relative funding for the foreign affairs budget—and transparency about how the spending is used—would contribute substantially to greater public support for such budgetary allocations.
- Finally, we found a clear preference for diplomats to lead in foreign policy, as opposed to military leaders. This suggests support for ambassadors and State Department officials abroad to assume a higher profile in crisis and non-crisis situations alike. It also suggests that senior officials can build support for American diplomacy by reaching out domestically to talk to—and listen to—the American public.
- Our report provides a glimpse into American public opinion about the Foreign Service. We hope that researchers, policymakers, and other stakeholders will be able to follow up on these findings to evaluate their validity and ongoing dynamics as the United States engages in vital relationships with the wider world.

---

[3] U.S. Department of State, "Remarks of Secretary of State Antony Blinken at the appointment of Ambassador Gina Abercrombie-Winstanley as Chief Diversity and Inclusion Officer," press release, April 12, 2021a.

# Contents

About This Report ............................................................................................................. iii
Summary ............................................................................................................................ v
Figures and Tables .......................................................................................................... xiii

**CHAPTER ONE**
**American Public Opinion and Foreign Policy** ............................................................. 1
    U.S. Global Engagement .................................................................................................. 2
    Public Knowledge and Perception of Foreign Policy Priorities ................................... 4
    Partisanship and U.S. Diplomacy ................................................................................... 5
    The Need for Further Research on Diplomacy and the State Department ................. 7

**CHAPTER TWO**
**Findings from the American Life Panel** ....................................................................... 9
    Survey Data and Analytic Approach .............................................................................. 9
    Comparison with Previous Surveys' Results ............................................................... 11
    Overall Views and Knowledge of U.S. Diplomats and Embassies ............................. 16
    Perceptions of Functions, Skills, and Qualities of U.S. Diplomats ........................... 20
    The Role of Diplomacy and the Foreign Service in National Security ..................... 26
    Perceptions of the Future of Diplomacy and the State Department ........................ 27
    Regional Differences in Attitudes ................................................................................ 30
    Summary of Survey Results .......................................................................................... 33

**CHAPTER THREE**
**Findings from In-Depth Focus Group Discussions** ................................................... 35
    Associations with the Term *American Diplomacy* ...................................................... 38
    Perceptions of the Success of American Diplomacy ................................................... 40
    Perceptions of Appropriate Goals of American Diplomacy ....................................... 41
    Importance of Tasks of American Diplomats ............................................................. 42
    Selection and Characteristics of Foreign Service Officers ......................................... 45
    The Future of American Diplomacy ............................................................................ 48
    Awareness of the Foreign Service ................................................................................. 50
    Views on Political Appointees Versus Career Diplomats .......................................... 52
    Summary of Focus Group Results ............................................................................... 53

**CHAPTER FOUR**
**Key Findings and Implications** ................................................................................... 55
    Key Findings ................................................................................................................... 55
    Implications ..................................................................................................................... 60
    Conclusion ....................................................................................................................... 63

**APPENDIXES**

A. American Life Panel Survey (Wave 1, 2020) ................................................. 65
B. American Life Panel Survey (Wave 2, 2021) ................................................. 71
C. **Selected Detailed Results** ................................................................ 77
D. **Focus Group Protocol** .................................................................... 91

**Abbreviations** ............................................................................... 97
**References** .................................................................................. 99

# Figures and Tables

## Figures

| | | |
|---|---|---|
| 1.1. | U.S. Role in World Affairs, 2021 Chicago Council on Global Affairs Survey | 4 |
| 2.1. | Percentage of Respondents Reporting "a Great Deal of Confidence" in Institutions, 2017–2021 | 14 |
| 2.2. | Percentage of Respondents Reporting That Entities Play a "Very Important" Role in Foreign Policy, 1974–2021 | 15 |
| 2.3. | Percentage of Respondents Reporting Overall Impression of American Diplomats and U.S. Embassies Abroad, 2020–2021 | 17 |
| 2.4. | Percentage of Respondents Reporting Overall Impression of American Diplomats and U.S. Embassies Abroad, by Gender, 2020–2021 | 17 |
| 2.5. | Percentage of Respondents Reporting Knowledge of Functions Performed by Diplomats, by Number Known | 18 |
| 2.6. | Percentage of Respondents Reporting Awareness of Diplomatic Functions, 2020 | 19 |
| 2.7. | Most Important Functions of Diplomats, by Percentage Overall, 2020 and 2021 | 21 |
| 2.8. | Most Important Skills of Diplomats, by Percentage Overall, 2020 and 2021 | 23 |
| 2.9. | Perceptions of Whether Diplomats Are Trustworthy and Politically Biased, by Percentage, 2020–2021 | 24 |
| 2.10. | Perceptions of Whether Diplomats Are Representative, by Percentage, 2020–2021 | 24 |
| 2.11. | Respondents' Perceived Efficacy of Career Versus Appointed Ambassadors, by Percentage, 2021 | 26 |
| 2.12. | Perceptions of Whether Diplomacy Contributes to National Security, by Percentage, 2020–2021 | 27 |
| 2.13. | Perceptions of Whether Diplomats or the Military Should Lead Efforts Abroad, by Percentage, 2020–2021 | 27 |
| 2.14. | Perceptions of Whether Face-to-Face Diplomacy Is Still Important in the Digital Age, by Percentage, 2020–2021 | 28 |
| 2.15. | Perceptions of the Adequacy of State Department Funding, by Percentage, 2001–2021 | 29 |
| 2.16. | Perceptions of the Adequacy of State Department Funding After Additional Information, by Percentage, 2020–2021 | 29 |
| 2.17. | U.S. Census Regions | 30 |
| 2.18. | Favorable Impressions of American Diplomats, by Census Region, 2020–2021 | 31 |
| 2.19. | Perceptions of the Importance of Promoting American Values Through Diplomacy, by Percentage, 2021 | 32 |

## Tables

| | | |
|---|---|---|
| 1.1. | Percentage Reporting That Foreign Policy Goals Should Be "Very Important" or "a Top Goal" in ANES, CCGA, and Pew Surveys, 2004–2021 | 6 |
| 2.1. | Longitudinal Sample Characteristics (Weighted) | 12 |
| 3.1. | Focus Group Characteristics | 36 |
| C.1. | Proportions and Means of Unweighted Sociodemographic and Other Background Variables, by Wave | 78 |
| C.2. | Results of Logistic Regressions for Increasing Perceived Importance of the Secretary of State in Determining Foreign Policy to "Very Important" in 2021 from Any Other Rating in 2020 | 79 |
| C.3. | Results of Logistic Regressions for Positive Overall Impression of American Diplomats and U.S. Embassies Abroad in 2020 | 81 |
| C.4. | Results of Ordinary Least Squares Regression for Sum of Number of Functions Performed by Diplomats Known by Respondents, 2020 | 83 |
| C.5. | Results of Logistic Regressions for Perceptions of American Diplomats as Trustworthy or Politically Biased, 2020 | 85 |
| C.6. | Results of Ordinary Least Squares Regression for Sum of Number of Roles That Career Ambassadors Were Considered More Effective at Than Appointed Ambassadors, 2021 | 87 |
| C.7. | Results of Logistic Regressions for Perceptions of American Diplomats as Trustworthy or Politically Biased, Controlling for Geographic Region, 2020 and 2021 | 89 |

CHAPTER ONE

# American Public Opinion and Foreign Policy

The U.S. State Department and American diplomats serving around the world play key roles in the development and implementation of U.S. foreign policy; represent and protect American interests and U.S. citizens; promote peace, security, and economic opportunities; and assist Americans traveling or living overseas. This report describes public attitudes toward diplomacy and diplomats.

The project takes as a starting point previous polling and studies of changing American attitudes toward engagement in the world, such as the respected series of polls for the Chicago Council on Global Affairs (CCGA) that span more than four decades.[1] For the most part, such polling focuses on the *what* of foreign policy—illuminating attitudes toward issues and questions such as the following: Should the United States be more engaged in world affairs, or should it withdraw?[2] Should the United States spend more or less on diplomacy?[3] What should foreign policy goals be?[4]

Our research adds insights on some of these questions but is primarily focused on the American public's opinions about the *who* and the *how* of diplomacy. Do Americans look favorably on their Foreign Service Officers (FSOs)? What are the most important functions that diplomats undertake? How should diplomats be selected? How much should the nation rely on political, non-career ambassadors?

For the U.S. State Department to become an effective leader in the making and implementation of foreign policy, financial and bipartisan support is needed, which requires steadfast

---

[1] The most recent in the series is Dina Smeltz, Ivo Daalder, Karl Friedhoff, Craig Kafura, and Emily Sullivan, *A Foreign Policy for the Middle Class—What Americans Think: Results of the 2021 Chicago Council Survey of American Public Opinion and U.S. Foreign Policy*, Chicago, Ill.: Lester Crown Center on U.S. Foreign Policy and Chicago Council on Global Affairs, 2021.

[2] For example, the CCGA surveys ask, "Do you think it will be best for the future of the country if we take an active part in world affairs or if we stay out of world affairs?"

[3] For example, Pew Research Center asks, "If you were making up the budget for the federal government next year, would you increase spending, decrease spending, or keep spending the same for the State Department and American Embassies?"

[4] For example, CCGA and the American National Election Studies (ANES) ask, "Below is a list of possible foreign policy goals that the United States might have. For each one, please select whether you think that it should be a very important foreign policy goal of the United States, a somewhat important foreign policy goal, or not an important goal at all."

support from the American people.[5] It is unclear, however, whether (or to what degree) Americans see the connection between having a strong State Department and their own prosperity, security, and well-being. The lack of awareness may be due to lack of public appreciation for American diplomacy and its role in advancing the interests of the American public.[6]

The recent Belfer Center report, *A U.S. Diplomatic Service for the 21st Century*, recommends that efforts to reform the State Department should be bipartisan.[7] A bipartisan legislative package to renew American leadership abroad has recently been introduced that calls for the revitalization of American diplomacy, leadership, and investments globally.[8] The report from the Belfer Center argues that "just as the United States succeeded in renewing both the military and intelligence agencies in recent decades, we must now do the same for our diplomats and diplomacy."[9] It is not known whether the public knows about such efforts or how important the public considers this issue to be.

This section notes several key areas of existing research about American public opinion and attitudes toward the State Department, diplomacy, and American diplomats and identifies gaps and needs for future research and policy analysis. Subsequent chapters present the findings of surveys that we administered in May 2020 and June 2021 to a nationally representative sample of Americans, as well as insights from 14 focus groups we conducted across the country. A final chapter summarizes the key findings and policy implications of the surveys and focus groups we conducted.

Our 2020 and 2021 ALP questionnaires and detailed statistical results from key survey data analyses are provided in Appendixes A, B, and C, respectively, with the protocol that our moderators used for the focus groups included in Appendix D.

# U.S. Global Engagement

CCGA has conducted regular surveys of American public attitudes toward foreign policy and international issues for over 45 years. The surveys were conducted every four years begin-

---

[5] Shannon W. Caudill, Andrew M. Leonard, and Richard D. Thresher, "Interagency Leadership: The Case for Strengthening the Department of State," *American Diplomacy*, April 2008.

[6] *The Economist*, "The Dereliction of American Diplomacy," August 15, 2020.

[7] Nicholas Burns, Marc Grossman, and Marcie Ries, *American Diplomacy Project: A U.S. Diplomatic Service for the 21st Century*, Cambridge, Mass.: Belfer Center for Science and International Affairs, Harvard Kennedy School, November 2020.

[8] House Foreign Affairs Committee, "Meeks Introduces Legislative Package to Renew American Leadership Abroad in Face of China Challenge," press release, Washington, D.C., May 25, 2021.

[9] Burns, Grossman, and Ries, 2020.

ning in 1974[10] and biennially since 2002.[11] Beginning with the 2014 report, the surveys are annual.[12]

The 2021 CCGA survey found that Americans generally endorse the idea that domestic investments add to American influence abroad.[13] Improving public education and strengthening democracy at home were the two factors considered most important to the United States remaining influential.[14] Furthermore, the report found that 68 percent of Americans "say that globalization is mostly good for the United States" and do not see "trade and globalization as sources of unfairness in American life." The 2021 CCGA report echoed findings from prior studies, such as its *America Engaged* report of 2018, which revealed that Americans think that global engagement, "being admired," and international trade advance their security and prosperity and that Americans want the United States to remain engaged with the world (Figure 1.1).[15] More than 90 percent of Americans support multilateral diplomacy and say that it is more effective for the United States to work with other countries to achieve its foreign policy goals.[16] Except for just after the September 11 attacks, most Americans over the past two decades have supported active U.S. engagement in world affairs. While such data show increasing support for diplomacy,[17] the budget for the State Department has been cut substantially over the past ten years.[18] Furthermore, as the 2021 CCGA report shows, "a majority of Americans (69 percent) wants the United States to play a shared leadership role in the world."

---

[10] John E. Rielly, ed., *American Public Opinion and U.S. Foreign Policy 1975*, Chicago, Ill.: Chicago Council on Foreign Relations, 1975.

[11] Marshall M. Bouton and Benjamin I. Pahe, *Worldviews 2002: American Public Opinion & Foreign Policy*, Chicago, Ill.: Chicago Council on Global Affairs, October 1, 2002.

[12] Dina Smeltz, Ivo Daalder, and Craig Kafura, *Foreign Policy in the Age of Retrenchment: Results of the 2014 Chicago Council Survey of American Public Opinion and U.S. Foreign Policy*, Chicago, Ill.: Chicago Council on Global Affairs, 2014.

[13] As evinced in responses to the question "Please indicate how important the following factors are to the United States remaining influential on the global stage" (Smeltz et al., 2021, p. 4).

[14] Smeltz et al., 2021, p. 4.

[15] As evinced in reply to the question "Do you think it will be best for the future of the country if we take an active part in world affairs or if we stay out of world affairs?" (Dina Smeltz, Ivo Daalder, Karl Friedhoff, Craig Kafura, and Lily Wojtowicz, *2018 Chicago Council Survey—America Engaged: American Public Opinion and U.S. Foreign Policy*, Chicago, Ill.: Lester Crown Center on U.S. Foreign Policy and Chicago Council on Global Affairs, 2018, p. 2). See also Jackie Smith, Marina Karides, Marc Becker, Dorval Brunelle, Christopher Chase-Dunn, and Donatella Della Porta, *Global Democracy and the World Social Forums*, 2nd ed., Abingdon, UK: Routledge, 2014.

[16] As evinced in reply to the question "When dealing with international problems, the United States should be more willing to make decisions within the United Nations even if this means that the United States will sometimes have to go along with a policy that is not its first choice" (Smeltz et al., 2018, p. 13).

[17] Pew Research Center, "6. Views of Foreign Policy," webpage, December 17, 2019.

[18] U.S. Department of State, "International Affairs Budgets," webpage, undated.

**FIGURE 1.1**
**U.S. Role in World Affairs, 2021 Chicago Council on Global Affairs Survey**

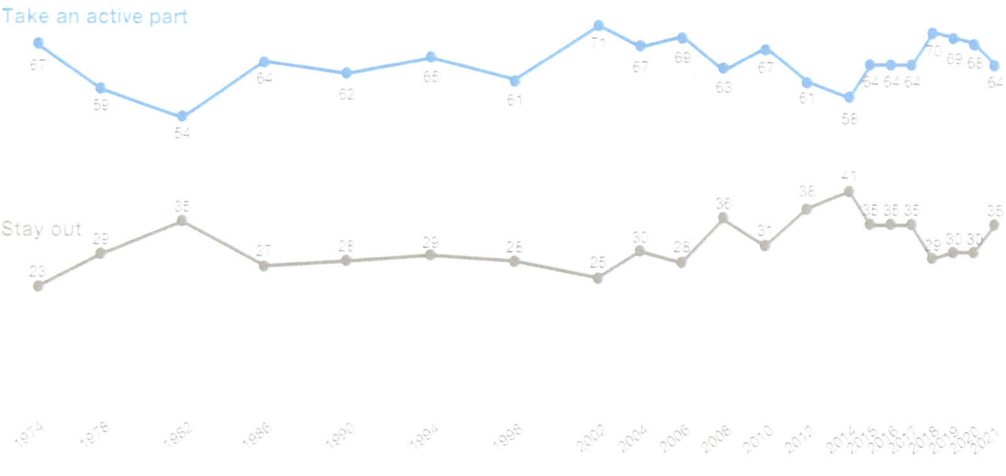

Take an active part
67, 59, 54, 64, 62, 65, 61, 71, 67, 69, 63, 67, 61, 58, 64, 64, 64, 70, 69, 65, 64

Stay out
23, 29, 35, 27, 25, 29, 25, 25, 36, 30, 26, 31, 36, 41, 35, 35, 35, 29, 30, 30, 35

SOURCE: Adapted from Smeltz et al., 2021.
NOTE: This figure shows the percentages of responses to the question "Do you think it will be best for the future of the country if we take an active part in world affairs or if we stay out of world affairs?"

## Public Knowledge and Perception of Foreign Policy Priorities

There is a substantial literature documenting that many Americans are poorly informed about foreign affairs[19] and that this lack of knowledge translates into low public engagement with foreign policy.[20] At the same time, this view is being challenged by work that indicates that the public holds reasonably sensible and nuanced views on foreign policies[21] and that attitudes about foreign affairs are partly derived from political elites who provide cues to the poorly informed public.[22]

---

[19] See, e.g., Michael X. Delli Carpini and Scott Keeter, *What Americans Know About Politics and Why It Matters*, New Haven, Conn.: Yale University Press, 1996. Also see Ole R. Holsti, *Public Opinion and American Foreign Policy*, revised edition, Ann Arbor, Mich.: University of Michigan Press, 2004.

[20] See, e.g., Michael X. Delli Carpini, Scott Keeter, and Sharon Webb, "The Impact of Presidential Debates," in Pippa Norris, ed., *Politics and the Press: The News Media and Their Influences*, Boulder, Colo.: Rienner, 1997. Also see Ole R. Holsti and James N. Rosenau, *American Leadership in World Affairs: Vietnam and the Breakdown of Consensus*, Boston: Allen & Unwin, 1984, and Charles W. Ostrom and Brian L. Job, "The President and the Political Use of Force," *American Political Science Review*, Vol. 80, No. 2, 1986.

[21] For example, John H. Aldrich, Christopher Gelpi, Peter Feaver, Jason Reifler, and Kristin Thompson Sharp, "Foreign Policy and the Electoral Connection," *Annual Review of Political Science*, Vol. 9, 2006.

[22] Matthew A. Baum and Tim Groeling, "Shot by the Messenger: Partisan Cues and Public Opinion Regarding National Security and War," *Political Behavior*, Vol. 31, No. 2, June 2009; Adam J. Berinsky, *Silent Voices: Opinion Polls and Political Participation in America*, Princeton, N.J.: Princeton University Press, 2004; Robert Johns, "Tracing Foreign Policy Decisions: A Study of Citizens' Use of Heuristics," *British Journal of Politics and International Relations*, Vol. 11, No. 4, 2009.

Since 1971, the General Social Survey conducted by NORC at the University of Chicago has only once directly asked respondents to "Please indicate whether you are very informed, somewhat informed, neither informed nor uninformed, somewhat uninformed, or very uninformed about foreign policy."[23] While 7 percent of respondents indicated that they were very informed, and 44 percent indicated that they were somewhat informed, 31 percent of respondents indicated they were somewhat or very uninformed.[24]

Despite this, the public generally holds clear views of the importance of a range of foreign policy priorities, which have been tracked by a number of groups at various times, including CCGA, ANES, and Pew Research Center, among others. Table 1.1 presents trends in the percentage of Americans who reported that specific foreign policy goals should be "very important" (ANES and CCGA)[25] or "a top goal" (Pew).[26] Note that the table includes the common subset of policy goals across the various sources and is not an exhaustive list of all goals from each survey.[27] The consistency in ordinal ranking of importance of each of the listed goals between 2004 and 2021 is notable across surveys and sources.

## Partisanship and U.S. Diplomacy

The "common holding . . . that typical Americans know little (and care less) about foreign policy"[28] may need to be reconsidered in the context of greatly expanded sources of media and information,[29] as well as increasing political party polarization on many foreign policy issues. When issues become contested among partisan elites, Americans more easily form opinions about those issues, and they internalize their party's position as their own preferred position.[30]

---

[23] Tom W. Smith, Michael Davern, Jeremy Freese, and Stephen L. Morgan, "General Social Survey, 2006," machine-readable data file, Chicago, Ill.: NORC, 2019.

[24] 17 percent indicated that they were neither informed nor uninformed. Results are weighted.

[25] ANES and CCGA ask, "Should [each goal] be a very important foreign policy goal, somewhat important foreign policy goal, or not an important foreign policy goal at all?"

[26] Pew asks, "Below is a list of possible foreign policy goals that the United States might have. For each one, please select whether you think that it should be a very important foreign policy goal of the United States, a somewhat important foreign policy goal, or not an important goal at all?"

[27] All goals that appear in at least two different sources are included. ANES included this question only in 2004 and 2008. Pew and CCGA have asked the question in additional years (not shown).

[28] Matthew A. Baum and Philip B. K. Potter, "Media, Public Opinion, and Foreign Policy in the Age of Social Media," *Journal of Politics*, Vol. 81, No. 2, 2019.

[29] Baum and Potter, 2019; Amnon Cavari and Guy Freedman, "Partisan Cues and Opinion Formation on Foreign Policy," *American Politics Research*, Vol. 47, No. 1, 2019; Gabriel S. Lenz, "Learning and Opinion Change, Not Priming: Reconsidering the Priming Hypothesis," *American Journal of Political Science*, Vol. 53, No. 4, October 2009.

[30] Baum and Groeling, 2009.

**TABLE 1.1**

**Percentage Reporting That Foreign Policy Goals Should Be "Very Important" or "a Top Goal" in ANES, CCGA, and Pew Surveys, 2004–2021**

| Foreign Policy Goal | ANES | | CCGA | | | | Pew |
|---|---|---|---|---|---|---|---|
| | 2004 | 2008 | 2006 | 2010 | 2015 | 2021 | 2021 |
| Protecting the jobs of American workers | 86 | 89 | 76 | 79 | 73 | 79 | 75 |
| Preventing the spread of nuclear weapons | 86 | 83 | 74 | 73 | 72 | 75 | 64 |
| Combating international terrorism | 81 | 77 | 72 | 69 | 65 | 66 | 71 |
| Combating world hunger | 59 | 59 | 43 | 42 | 42 | 50 | — |
| Controlling and reducing illegal immigration | 58 | 57 | 58 | 59 | 52 | 50 | 38 |
| Strengthening the United Nations | 48 | 42 | 40 | 37 | — | — | 30 |
| Promoting and defending human rights in other countries | 43 | 35 | 28 | 30 | 30 | 41 | 34 |
| Helping bring a democratic form of government to other nations | 22 | 18 | 17 | 19 | — | 18 | 20 |

NOTES: ANES and CCGA ask, "Should [each goal] be a very important foreign policy goal, somewhat important foreign policy goal, or not an important foreign policy goal at all?" while Pew asks, "Below is a list of possible foreign policy goals that the United States might have. For each one, please select whether you think that it should be a very important foreign policy goal of the United States, a somewhat important foreign policy goal, or not an important goal at all?"
SOURCES: ANES, undated. CCGA: Bouton et al., 2006; Bouton et al., 2010; Smeltz et al., 2015; and Smeltz et al., 2021. Pew Research Center, 2021.

Support for global engagement is not a heavily partisan matter, as noted by the CCGA 2020 report,[31] fielded in the midst of the 2020 presidential campaign. Similarly, the Eurasia Group Foundation's 2020 report entitled *Diplomacy and Restraint* concluded that "[p]artisan differences in attitudes about global engagement were smaller than might be expected."[32]

Yet the 2020 CCGA report, *Divided We Stand*, found a growing divide on some specific foreign policies based on political affiliation. For example, it showed that Democrats were more likely to support international cooperation and collaboration, and it reveals various trends where divergence of opinions is expected to grow based on party affiliations.[33] Similarly, a 2021 Pew Research Center survey highlighted partisan differences in support for a

---

[31] Dina Smeltz, Ivo Daalder, Karl Friedhoff, Craig Kafura, and Brendan Helm, *Divided We Stand: Democrats and Republicans Diverge on U.S. Foreign Policy, Results of the 2020 Chicago Council Survey of American Public Opinion and U.S. Foreign Policy*, Chicago, Ill.: Lester Crown Center on U.S. Foreign Policy and Chicago Council on Global Affairs, 2020, pp. 9–10.

[32] Mark Hannah and Caroline Gray, *Diplomacy & Restraint: The Worldview of American Voters*, New York: Eurasia Group Foundation, September 2020.

[33] Smeltz et al., 2020, pp. 15–17.

range of foreign policy goals (including those in Table 1.1).[34] Pew concluded, consistent with CCGA, that Democrats were more likely than Republicans to prioritize outward-facing foreign policy goals (such as dealing with global climate change, reducing the spread of infectious diseases, and improving relationships with our allies), while Republicans were more likely to prioritize inward goals (such as maintaining the U.S. military advantage, protecting the jobs of American workers, and reducing illegal immigration into the United States).

## The Need for Further Research on Diplomacy and the State Department

While there are survey data tracking perceptions of the importance of specific foreign policy goals and broader questions about the importance of global engagement, existing data are insufficient to gain insight into how Americans specifically view diplomacy and international affairs, the role of U.S. diplomats, or what they think of the diplomats themselves.

The data reviewed in this section show that Americans are concerned about national security and economic prosperity, but it is unclear whether people are informed about how and why diplomacy works to secure such goals and advance their interests. Although this chapter did not review all foreign policy topics covered by various surveys, existing survey data are broadly consistent in that they lack concrete evidence on how the American people view U.S. embassies or diplomats abroad. Better data to capture public attitudes toward the Department of State and the public's understanding of the role of American diplomacy and diplomats in national security could inform policies and strategies for enhancing U.S. statecraft. Our study aimed to address these issues.

---

[34] Mara Mordecai and Moira Fagan, "How U.S. Views on Foreign Policy and International Cooperation Are Linked," Washington, D.C.: Pew Research Center, May 5, 2021.

CHAPTER TWO

# Findings from the American Life Panel

As identified in the previous chapter, information is sparse about the general public's knowledge and perceptions of the Foreign Service in general and American diplomats in particular. In this chapter, we present results from the first nationally representative surveys on these issues in order to gauge public opinion on a range of topics to illuminate respondents' baseline knowledge of American diplomatic practices and capabilities, the existence and principles of operation of the Foreign Service, the frequency of respondents' interactions with embassies or Foreign Service personnel in person or via websites, and opinions about resourcing diplomacy (itself and relative to other forms of national security spending). In this chapter, we describe the data source and sample; compare results with earlier data on the importance of and confidence in the State Department; present overall views and knowledge of American diplomats and U.S. embassies; summarize the public's views on the functions, skills, and qualities of diplomats; examine views expressed by respondents on diplomacy and national security; and offer the views expressed on the future of diplomacy.

## Survey Data and Analytic Approach

This portion of the project analysis relies on two surveys of 1,829 members of the RAND American Life Panel (ALP) conducted in May/June 2020 and again in June/July 2021 about their perceptions of U.S. embassies abroad and the Americans who serve as diplomats in them. Surveying the same nationally representative sample at two time points, about a year apart, allowed us to measure baseline knowledge and attitudes and individual-level changes in those attitudes over time. This approach strengthens our ability to identify real changes in attitudes, rather than artifacts of differing groups of people at each time point.

The sample for this survey was randomly drawn from the larger ALP sample ages 24 and older.[1] The ALP is a nationally representative probability-sample-based internet panel

---

[1] An initial sample of 2,517 panel members was originally invited to participate in the survey, with a desired wave 1 sample size of 2,000 respondents. The survey was closed after two weeks, once 2,026 respondents (80.5 percent of all invited) completed the first survey. All 2,026 wave 1 respondents were invited to participate in the second wave, with 90.3 percent (1,829) completing the second survey. Wave 2 participation was statistically significantly lower for younger, lower-income, and non-Hispanic black individuals; neither political attitudes nor overall favorability of American diplomats predicted wave 2 nonparticipa-

of more than 5,000 U.S. adults who were age 18 or older at recruitment into the panel. ALP respondents are originally either sampled by random digit dial (landline and cell phone) or address-based sampling; individuals cannot otherwise volunteer to participate. A further advantage over most other internet panels is that the respondents to the ALP need not have internet access when they are initially recruited (RAND provides laptops and internet subscriptions if needed), reducing a potential source of bias.

Since January 2006, the ALP has fielded nearly 600 surveys on topics including financial decisionmaking, the effect of political events on self-reported well-being, joint retirement decisions, health decisionmaking, Social Security knowledge and expectations, measurement of health utility, voting preference in the presidential election, and more.[2] Data from all surveys are made publicly available to more than 600 clients and registered users from numerous institutions. As with other surveys, RAND weights responses to ensure that results are representative of the U.S. population, matching to the U.S. Census Bureau's Current Population Survey, with additional post-stratification to match the known voting behavior of the electorate in 2016.[3] Complete technical details of the ALP and its recruitment, retention, and weighting procedures are available elsewhere.[4]

The baseline ALP survey for this study included background questions about prior experience visiting or contacting a U.S. embassy or the State Department for help or information, as well as a range of questions regarding overall knowledge, impressions, and perceptions of American diplomats; skills and functions they may perform, and the relative importance of the role they play in shaping policies that benefit the United States compared with other institutions. Respondents were asked the same set of attitudinal questions one year later to assess individual-level changes in attitudes and beliefs over time. The second survey also included a handful of new items that were developed in response to the focus group session discussions with other participants that occurred after the baseline survey (described in Chapter Three).

---

tion. Unweighted demographic distributions of the complete wave 1 and wave 2 samples are provided in Appendix C.

[2] Response rates to any particular ALP survey are typically around 80 percent, depending on the length of the survey and the time in the field. Most participants respond within one week, but response rates rise to about 85 percent after one month. ALP member retention across years is between 93 and 94 percent per year.

[3] This known voting behavior is whether the respondent voted in the 2016 presidential election and whom they voted for. This information is matched to the national distribution of votes cast during the post-stratification step. The ability to account for the known underparticipation of politically conservative individuals in surveys is an important feature of the ALP in cases where the interview topics are potentially sensitive to partisan views.

[4] RAND American Life Panel, homepage, 2020; Michael S. Pollard and Joshua Mendelsohn, *Methodology of the 2016 RAND Presidential Election Panel Survey (PEPS)*, Santa Monica, Calif.: RAND Corporation, RR-1460-RC/UCLA, 2016; and Michael S. Pollard and Matthew D. Baird, *The RAND American Life Panel: Technical Description*, Santa Monica, Calif.: RAND Corporation, RR-1651, 2017.

## Sample Characteristics

Details of the variable coding and descriptive statistics are presented in Table 2.1, and wave 1 and 2 survey instruments are provided in Appendixes A and B, respectively. The analytic sample includes the respondents who participated in both waves. As noted, 90 percent of the baseline sample completed both waves. Wave 2 participation was statistically significantly lower for younger, lower-income, and non-Hispanic black individuals.[5] Note that liberal/conservative political ideological background, voting history, and baseline favorability of American diplomats were not associated with nonparticipation at wave 2.

More than half (55.2 percent) of the sample reported that they had a U.S. passport at the time of the first survey (2020).[6] Among those who indicated holding a passport, nearly three-quarters (73.7 percent) also reported that they had traveled outside of the United States within the past ten years. Overall, 5.7 percent of the sample indicated that they had visited a U.S. embassy for help or information, while 28.4 percent had visited a U.S. embassy website or state.gov for help or information.

Throughout the following presentation of survey results, findings shown in the figures are based on weighted survey results that reflect overall attitudes among American adults ages 24 and older. When discussing specific predictors of baseline (or changes in baseline) attitudes, results are assessed using ordinary least squares for continuous measures or logistic regression for binary measures, with a common set of sociodemographic and political partisanship variables used as predictors. Predictor variables include gender, race/ethnicity, age, level of education, income, rural/urban residence, marital status, whether or not the respondent voted in 2016, and political orientation (ranging from very liberal to very conservative).[7]

Overall change in attitudes from 2020 to 2021 was assessed by whether the change in sample mean or proportion was significantly different from 0 ($p < 0.05$).

## Comparison with Previous Surveys' Results

To help validate the RAND survey samples, we chose to ask a few questions that had been asked in other broadly representative surveys by CCGA. We took this approach in both waves of the ALP surveys.

---

[5] This result is based on logistic regression with survey weights.

[6] An *Economist*/YouGov poll in April 2021 indicated that 37 percent of adults ages 18+ had a valid and unexpired U.S. passport (Kathy Frankovic, "Only One-Third of Americans Have a Valid U.S. Passport," YouGov, April 21, 2021). The higher rate of passport possession among our sample may partly reflect our older sample.

[7] We also explored the potential for regional differences in addition to these variables, but they were broadly not statistically significant across the questions we assessed after controlling for other sociodemographics, as discussed below and in Appendix C.

**TABLE 2.1**
**Longitudinal Sample Characteristics (Weighted)**

| Variable | Percentage or Mean |
|---|---|
| Male | 44.6% |
| Female | 55.4% |
| Non-Hispanic white | 59.4% |
| Non-Hispanic black | 12.3% |
| Non-Hispanic other | 6.4% |
| Hispanic | 21.9% |
| Age (in years) | 50.1 |
| College degree or greater education | 29.5% |
| Income (in $1,000s) | 70.4 |
| Urban (population >50,000) | 79.8% |
| Rural (population <50,000) | 20.2% |
| Married | 57.7% |
| Voted in 2016 | 61.3% |
| Conservativism (range 1–5) (very liberal to very conservative) | 2.9 |
| Has ever visited a U.S. embassy | 5.7% |
| Has ever visited a U.S. embassy website or state.gov | 28.4% |
| Has passport and has traveled outside the United States in the past ten years | 73.7% |
| | N = 1,829 |

Respondents were asked about the level of confidence they "have in the ability of leaders in [a list of] institutions to shape policies that benefit the United States." CCGA asked this question in 2017 and 2018 to gauge public perception of key entities.[8] By asking the same question, we were able to extend the series of responses into 2020 and 2021. By asking these questions of the same respondents, we were also able to examine whether changes in confidence were occurring at the individual level, rather than reflecting changes in population composition more broadly.

---

[8] See Dina Smeltz, Ivo Daalder, Karl Friedhoff, and Craig Kafura, *Results of the 2017 Chicago Council Survey of American Public Opinion and U.S. Foreign Policy: What Americans Think About America First*, Chicago, Ill.: Chicago Council on Global Affairs, 2017.

Respondents also were presented with a list of nine institutions[9] and asked to rate their confidence in each using one of four options: "a great deal," "a fair amount," "not very much," or "no confidence at all." We replicated this wording and present the percentage reporting "a great deal" of confidence for 2020 and 2021, along with the prior CCGA data, in Figure 2.1.

The ALP data generally align with the CCGA data, although confidence in intelligence organizations and the State Department appears to be modestly higher in the ALP survey data. In regard to confidence in the State Department specifically, 24 percent of the adult population reported having "a great deal of confidence" in 2020. This contrasts with the 2017 and 2018 CCGA surveys, in which only 17 and 13 percent, respectively, reported "a great deal of confidence." While we are not able to identify whether the increase relative to the CCGA surveys is due to different samples or weighting approaches[10] as opposed to change over time, we are able to identify whether significant changes from 2020 to 2021 occurred among our respondents. The sole predictor of reporting a great deal of confidence in the State Department at baseline (2020) was age; older respondents were more likely to rate a high level of confidence. In 2021, there was a statistically significant six-percentage-point increase in the proportion of the population who reported a great deal of confidence in the State Department, equivalent to a 25-percent increase in the size of that group. People who changed their response to "a great deal" of confidence were older than others and more likely to live in an urban area.

Respondents were also asked, "How important a role do you think the following play in determining the foreign policy of the United States?" which is a question that has previously been asked in CCGA surveys in 1974, 1978, and 1982. Response options included "very important," "somewhat important," "hardly important," and "not sure." The list of entities asked about each survey varied slightly,[11] although the Secretary of State and the State Department were both included in each survey.

Figure 2.2 presents the time series in percentage of respondents answering "a very important role" in determining the foreign policy of the United States. Given the large period of time covered, there is remarkable consistency in the public perception of the importance of the State Department's role in this capacity, ranging from a low of 38 percent responding

---

[9] The list of institutions consists of the military, the U.S. State Department, intelligence agencies, Congress, think tanks, academia, the White House, large corporations, and the media. Note that respondents may not have understood what "intelligence agencies" refers to.

[10] The CCGA samples generally have higher proportions of younger, female, and lower-income and lower-educational attainment respondents than the ALP sample. CCGA weighting does not adjust for partisanship. See Smeltz et al., 2017.

[11] In all survey years, the list included the State Department as a whole, the Secretary of State, the President, Congress, the military, and public opinion. From 1978 on, the list also included American business, the Central Intelligence Agency (CIA), and the National Security Advisor. Note that in the survey question the abbreviation "CIA" is presented, and respondents may not have known or interpreted this as "Central Intelligence Agency."

**FIGURE 2.1**
**Percentage of Respondents Reporting "a Great Deal of Confidence" in Institutions, 2017–2021**

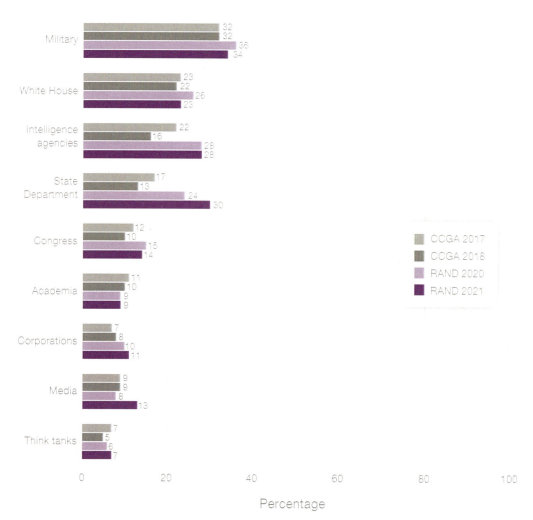

SOURCES: Analysis of CCGA and RAND ALP data. CCGA surveys are Smeltz et al., 2017, and Smeltz et al., 2018.
NOTES: This figure shows responses of "a great deal of confidence" to the question "Please tell me how much confidence you have in the ability of leaders in each of these institutions to shape policies that benefit the United States." Analysis includes survey weights.

**FIGURE 2.2**
**Percentage of Respondents Reporting That Entities Play a "Very Important" Role in Foreign Policy, 1974–2021**

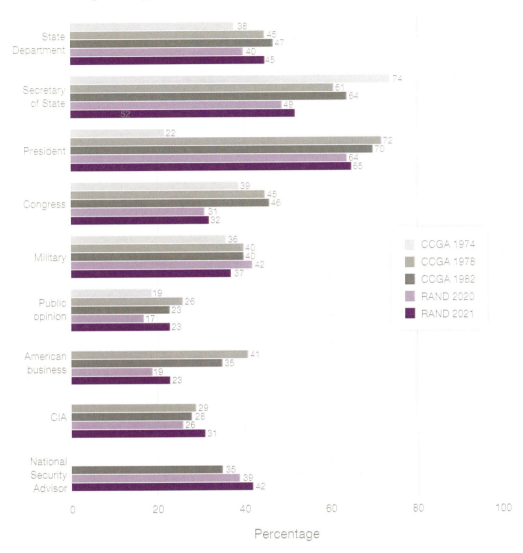

SOURCES: Analysis of CCGA and RAND ALP data. CCGA surveys are Rielly, 1975; Rielly, 1979; and Rielly, 1983.
NOTES: Responses of "a very important role" to the question "How important a role do you think the following currently play in determining the foreign policy of the United States—a very important role, a somewhat important role or hardly an important role at all?" are shown. Analysis includes survey weights.

"very important" in 1974 to a high of 47 percent in 1982. In contrast, the perception of importance of the Secretary of State ranges from 74 percent in 1974 to a low of 49 percent in 2020.

Older age was the only predictor of reporting "very important" for the Secretary of State in the RAND ALP data, but there were no significant predictors of perception of importance for the State Department as a whole. Again, we are able to measure whether there was individual-level change in the perception of importance by our respondents between 2020 and 2021.

While there were not significant changes in perceived importance of the Secretary of State or the State Department overall between 2020 and 2021, note that people who changed their perception of the importance of the State Department as a whole to "very important" in 2021 from something else in 2020 were more likely to be non-Hispanic, have higher incomes, live in urban areas, and be more liberal. This may in part reflect the change from a Republican to a Democratic administration between surveys. In terms of changes in importance of the Secretary of State specifically, individuals who were more likely to change their perception to "very important" from something else were more likely to be older, have a college degree and higher income, and be an urban resident, but political ideology was not a significant predictor.

## Overall Views and Knowledge of U.S. Diplomats and Embassies

Near the beginning of the survey, after being asked whether they held a U.S. passport, whether they had traveled outside the United States in the past ten years, and whether they had ever contacted an embassy abroad, respondents were asked about their "overall impression of American diplomats and U.S. embassies abroad," with response options ranging from "very favorable" to "very negative," as well as a "no opinion" option. At both timepoints of the survey administration, a substantial proportion reported having "no opinion," but attitudes otherwise were generally neutral or positive (Figure 2.3). Negative views were held by a small minority of respondents. There was no significant change in attitudes between 2020 and 2021. These patterns are broadly consistent across many of the topics we asked about in the survey: Large proportions reported no or neutral opinions, followed by positive sentiment, and with little or no change over time.

A similarly consistent pattern across topics is that men were generally both more likely to report having an opinion, and more likely to report a positive opinion, than women. For example, 26 percent of women and 15 percent of men indicated that they had no opinion on American diplomats in 2020, while 27 percent of women and 42 percent of men reported a favorable opinion (Figure 2.4). Individuals with a college degree or higher level of education, and people who voted in 2016, were also significantly more likely than others to report

## FIGURE 2.3
**Percentage of Respondents Reporting Overall Impression of American Diplomats and U.S. Embassies Abroad, 2020–2021**

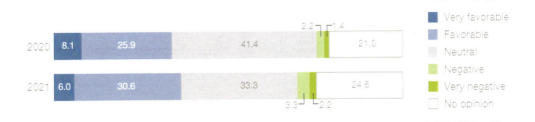

SOURCE: Analysis of RAND ALP data.
NOTE: Analysis includes survey weights.

## FIGURE 2.4
**Percentage of Respondents Reporting Overall Impression of American Diplomats and U.S. Embassies Abroad, by Gender, 2020–2021**

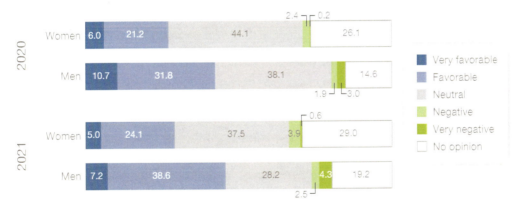

SOURCE: Analysis of RAND ALP data.
NOTE: Analysis includes survey weights.

"favorable" or "very favorable" impressions.[12] As noted throughout the discussion of results, these characteristics are part of a larger group of characteristics that tended to be positively linked to perceptions and attitudes about the Foreign Service and U.S. diplomats in the survey: higher education, participation in voting, male gender, and, slightly less frequently, higher age and income. Also as detailed below, political views (along a very liberal to very conservative continuum) were generally not linked to perceptions of overall favorability of or

---

[12] Based on logistic regression.

confidence in the State Department but were linked to perceptions of what types of characteristics diplomats should have and the tasks that they do.

Under the initial assumption that most people are not familiar with the Foreign Service or the functions of diplomats, and to help provide context for subsequent questions, respondents were then presented with a list of seven functions that American diplomats abroad perform.[13] Respondents were asked to identify which of the items they already knew diplomats perform and then were asked to identify which three functions from the list that they felt were the most important. The list included the following functions:

- Help U.S. citizens traveling or living abroad who are in trouble (e.g., in case of arrest, disaster, or other emergencies).
- Advance American interests with foreign governments and foreign citizens, including on national security matters.
- Report on developments in the countries where they are located that may affect the United States.
- Negotiate treaties and agreements.
- Help U.S. companies and farmers sell American products.
- Decide on applications for visas for travel to the United States.
- Promote and explain U.S. values and culture to encourage positive views of the United States and the American people.

Figure 2.5 presents the distribution of the number of items that respondents indicated that they already knew from the list. The mean number of functions that respondents reported already knowing was 4.4 out of a possible 7, with more than 10 percent of the sample unaware of any of the functions. Men, older respondents, those with a college degree, and people who voted in 2016 reported being aware of a higher number of functions.

Figure 2.6 presents how commonly known each function was in the 2020 survey. Helping citizens and reporting on developments in other countries topped the list, with at least three-quarters of adults already aware of these functions. The diplomatic function of negotiating

**FIGURE 2.5**

**Percentage of Respondents Reporting Knowledge of Functions Performed by Diplomats, by Number Known**

SOURCE: Analysis of RAND ALP data.
NOTE: Analysis includes survey weights.

---

[13] The items in the list were presented in random order to reduce ordering effects in the responses.

**FIGURE 2.6**
**Percentage of Respondents Reporting Awareness of Diplomatic Functions, 2020**

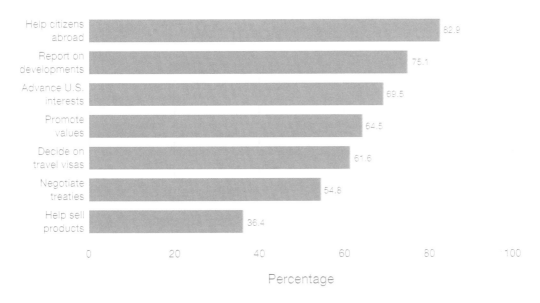

SOURCE: Analysis of RAND ALP data.
NOTE: Analysis includes survey weights.

treaties was known by only slightly more than half of the respondents, while helping American companies and farmers sell products was known by barely one-third of the respondents.

Also note that the number of items that respondents reported being aware of was positively associated with reporting a favorable or very favorable impression of American diplomats, above and beyond the sociodemographic factors identified above.[14] This was broadly true for most of the subsequent survey items as well; greater knowledge tended to be associated with responses that were generally favorable toward the Foreign Service or diplomats.[15] Also note that the respondents who reported low knowledge scores tended to respond "no opinion" to subsequent items in the surveys.[16]

---

[14] In a logistic regression; see Appendix Table C.3.

[15] However, higher knowledge scores were also associated with greater likelihood of a perception that diplomats were politically biased. This topic is discussed below.

[16] However, as shown in Appendix Table C.3, inclusion of the knowledge measure as a background predictor of attitudes did not impact the substantive links between other background predictors.

# Perceptions of Functions, Skills, and Qualities of U.S. Diplomats

Respondents were then asked to identify up to three of what they believed to be the most important functions that diplomats perform from an expanded list of functions, again presented in random order:

- Advance American interests with foreign governments.
- Help U.S. citizens in trouble.
- Help businesses sell U.S. products.
- Decide who can travel to the United States.
- Promote U.S. values and culture.
- Negotiate treaties and agreements.
- Work to fight international crime, drug trafficking, and terrorism.
- Promote scientific cooperation against global threats, such as pandemics.
- Represent the United States in the United Nations and other international organizations.

The percentage of respondents indicating that a function was among their perception of the top three most important functions performed by American diplomats is presented for both 2020 and 2021 in Figure 2.7. "Helping citizens" and "advancing U.S. interests with foreign governments" clearly and consistently represent the two functions perceived as most important. Conversely, "promoting scientific cooperation" and "helping sell U.S. products" were consistently perceived to be important by the smallest percentage of respondents. The perceptions of important functions were shared by respondents regardless of their overall favorable or unfavorable impression of American diplomats, with the exception that "advancing U.S. interests" was thought to be important by significantly more people who had favorable impressions than unfavorable ones (54 percent versus 33 percent in 2020, and 64 percent versus 38 percent in 2021, respectively). The functions that individual respondents reported already having knowledge of (in Figure 2.6) were also correlated with the functions that they identified as most important, suggesting an overlap between what respondents already knew and what they believed to be important.

Demographic factors were associated with respondents who rated functions as important.

Older individuals were more likely than others to rate "advancing interests" and "promoting values" as important, while younger individuals were more likely than others to rate "negotiating" as important. Individuals with higher incomes and/or education were more likely than others to report that "advancing interests," "promoting values," and "negotiating" were important, while those with lower incomes or educational attainment were more likely than others to rate "helping sell products," "determining visas," and "fighting crime and terrorism" as important. One interpretation of these patterns is that those with higher socioeconomic status view diplomats as having important proactive outreach functions, whereas

**FIGURE 2.7**
**Most Important Functions of Diplomats, by Percentage Overall, 2020 and 2021**

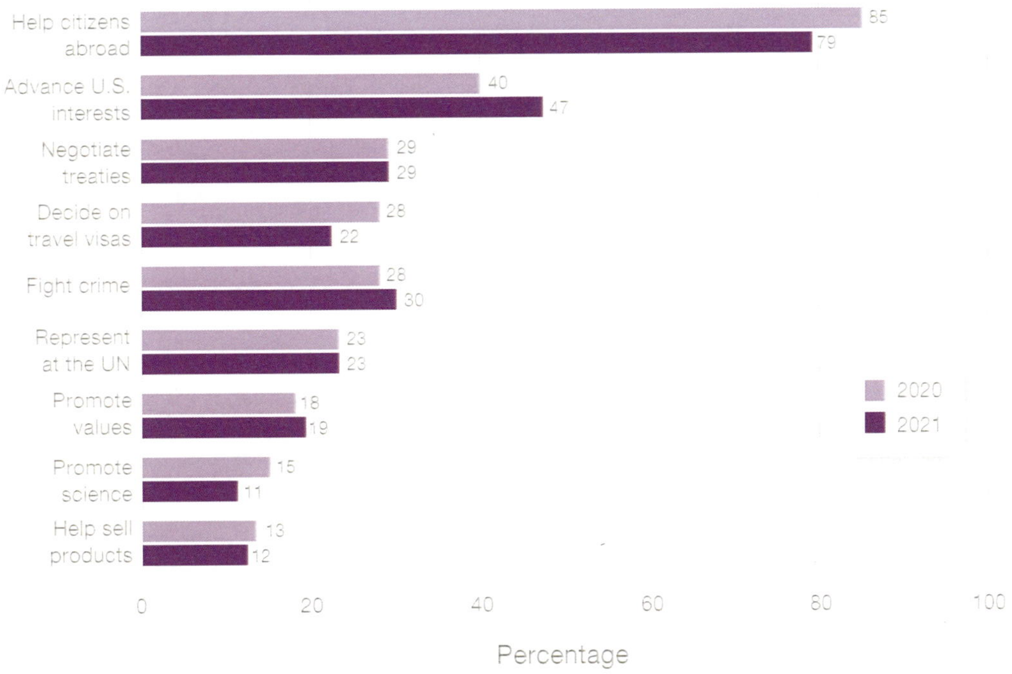

| Function | 2020 | 2021 |
|---|---|---|
| Help citizens abroad | 85 | 79 |
| Advance U.S. interests | 40 | 47 |
| Negotiate treaties | 29 | 29 |
| Decide on travel visas | 28 | 22 |
| Fight crime | 26 | 30 |
| Represent at the UN | 23 | 23 |
| Promote values | 18 | 19 |
| Promote science | 15 | 11 |
| Help sell products | 13 | 12 |

SOURCE: Analysis of RAND ALP data.
NOTE: Analysis includes survey weights.

lower socioeconomic groups view diplomats as having more important defensive or protective functions.

There were also several statistically significant changes in the functions that were rated most highly between 2020 and 2021. "Advancing U.S. interests with foreign governments" was selected as important by more people overall and by more people with a favorable impression of the Foreign Service in 2021 than in 2020. However, "helping citizens abroad," "determining travel visas," and "promoting scientific cooperation" was viewed as important by smaller numbers of people overall in 2021 compared with 2020. "Helping citizens abroad" also declined in importance for those with an unfavorable view. These shifts may be surprising given the increasing severity of the coronavirus pandemic in the time between survey administrations, potentially making these issues increasingly relevant. On the other hand, the decline may reflect a pandemic-related reduction in travel or travel plans. Additional demographic patterns that emerged include the following: Men were more likely than women to change their views between the two years. People who voted in 2016 were more likely than nonvoters to prioritize "advance interests" and deprioritize "scientific cooperation." Liberal respondents were more likely than conservative respondents to remove "scientific cooperation" from the functions of highest importance, while those with lower incomes were more likely to drop "travel visas" from that list.

After identifying what diplomatic functions respondents believed were the most important, respondents were asked a similar question about the two most important skills for diplomats to have. They were again presented with a randomly ordered list of the following items:[17]

- success in advancing U.S. interests
- understanding of global affairs
- language fluency
- negotiating skill
- bravery in the face of danger
- discipline in following instructions
- skill in public speaking/press affairs
- familiarity with U.S. politics
- empathy.[18]

The proportion of respondents indicating that a skill was among their top two most important skills for diplomats to have is presented for 2020 and 2021 in Figure 2.8. As with important functions, respondents clearly identified a few important skills and a few that were clearly viewed as much less important, with the rest ranked closely together in between. "Understanding of global affairs" and "negotiating skill" were consistently rated as the two most important skills for diplomats, while "public speaking," "bravery," "discipline in following instructions," and "empathy" all clustered at the low end of importance.

Perception of important skills was linked to several sociodemographic characteristics. "Success in advancing U.S. interests" was viewed as more important by older and rural individuals, while urban individuals were more likely than others to rate "familiarity with U.S. politics" highly. Younger respondents were more likely than older ones to rate "empathy" as an important skill. Respondents with higher incomes and educational attainment were associated with placing high importance on "understanding global affairs," while lower socioeconomic groups were more likely to prioritize "language skill," "bravery," "empathy," and an "understanding of U.S. politics." In contrast with changes over time in the perception of important *functions*, there were no significant changes in the perceptions of important *skills* between 2020 and 2021. This suggests that although the public view of the *functions* that diplomats perform changes over time in response to changing global and domestic context,

---

[17] Items were initially identified by Ambassador (Ret.) Charles Ries as a subject-matter expert and finalized by the entire research team. A write-in option was also provided for respondents to identify other unlisted functions but was used by less than 1 percent of respondents in either wave and was not considered further in the analysis.

[18] Empathy was not included in the 2020 survey but was added in response to several focus group discussions of important skills that mentioned it.

FIGURE 2.8
**Most Important Skills of Diplomats, by Percentage Overall, 2020 and 2021**

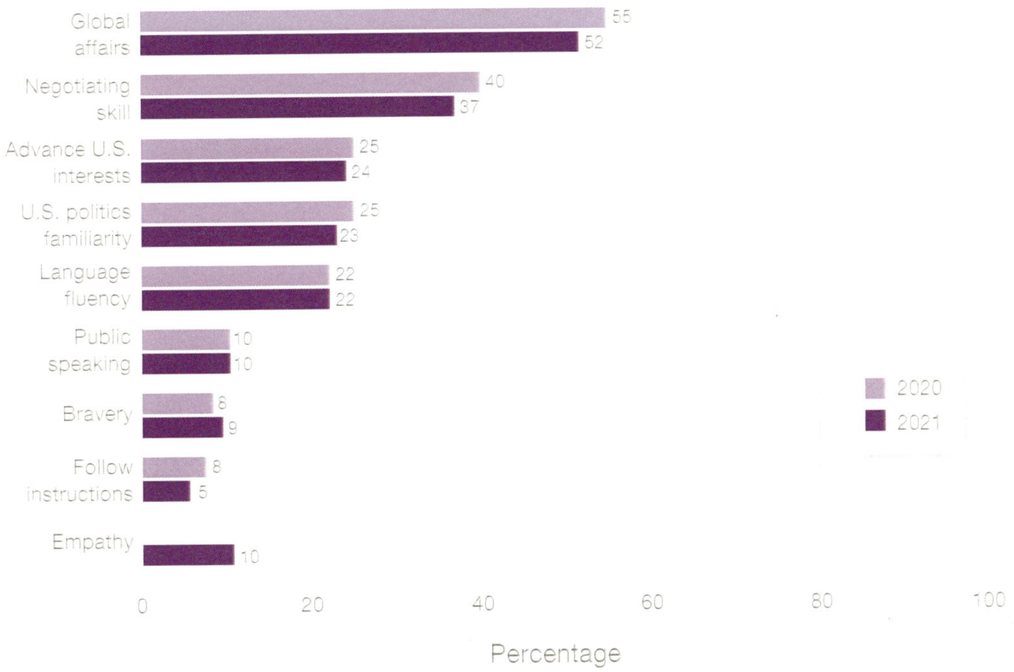

| Skill | 2020 | 2021 |
|---|---|---|
| Global affairs | 55 | 52 |
| Negotiating skill | 40 | 37 |
| Advance U.S. interests | 25 | 24 |
| U.S. politics familiarity | 25 | 23 |
| Language fluency | 22 | 22 |
| Public speaking | 10 | 10 |
| Bravery | 8 | 9 |
| Follow instructions | 8 | 5 |
| Empathy | | 10 |

SOURCE: Analysis of RAND ALP data.
NOTE: Analysis includes survey weights.

the views of *skills* that diplomats should have are less changeable, with "understanding of global affairs" and "negotiating skills" being consistently important regardless of functions performed.

In addition to sociodemographic characteristics, political ideology and political participation were associated with the perception of important functions and skills. More-liberal individuals prioritized "promoting scientific cooperation against global threats" and "understanding of global affairs," while more-conservative individuals prioritized "familiarity with U.S. politics," "fighting international crime and terrorism," and "discipline in following instructions." Those who were voters in 2016 prioritized "promoting U.S. values and culture" and "empathy," while those who did not vote in 2016 prioritized "helping U.S. citizens abroad" and "advancing American interests."

Respondents were also asked whether they considered American diplomats to be (1) trustworthy, (2) politically biased, and (3) representative of the United States in terms of racial and gender diversity and regional socioeconomic backgrounds. Once again, a substantial proportion of respondents had no opinion on these issues, but among those with opinions, similar proportions of respondents reported that they considered American diplomats to be trustworthy but also politically biased (Figure 2.9). Respondents with higher educational attainment and higher incomes were more likely to report a perception of trustworthiness than others. The only significant predictor of perceptions of political bias was level of knowledge (those with greater knowledge of diplomatic functions were also more likely to believe that diplomats were politically biased). Individuals who viewed diplomats as politically biased were much more likely than others to also believe they were not trustworthy.

In contrast with the stability in perceptions identified so far, in 2021 there was a significant increase in the proportion of respondents who did not believe that American diplomats are broadly representative (Figure 2.10). While most respondents in 2020 and 2021 indicated that they had no opinion, there was a statistically significant 8-percentage-point increase in the belief that diplomats were not representative, which equates to a 43-percent increase in the overall size of the group. While individuals with college degrees and Hispanic and other race individuals were more likely to believe that diplomats were not representative in 2020,

**FIGURE 2.9**

**Perceptions of Whether Diplomats Are Trustworthy and Politically Biased, by Percentage, 2020–2021**

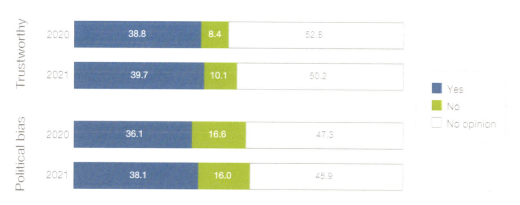

SOURCE: Analysis of RAND ALP data.
NOTE: Analysis includes survey weights.

**FIGURE 2.10**

**Perceptions of Whether Diplomats Are Representative, by Percentage, 2020–2021**

SOURCE: Analysis of RAND ALP data.
NOTE: Analysis includes survey weights.

women, Hispanic and other race individuals, married individuals, and more-conservative individuals were more likely than others to report an increase in their perception that diplomats were not representative in 2021.

## Additional Questions in 2021

During the focus group sessions (described in the next chapter), the distinction between career diplomats and political appointees was frequently brought up unprompted by the participants. In order to evaluate how widespread this concern is among Americans, we added a question to the 2021 nationwide ALP survey. Survey respondents were presented with the following information and question:

> The United States has two types of ambassadors: 1) professional career diplomats, who are selected through a series of written and oral exams, and have different assignments for 20 years or more before their nomination, and 2) political appointees nominated by the President, who come from varying backgrounds and generally serve only during the President's term and resign when a new president is inaugurated. As ambassadors, both career diplomats and political appointees are personal representatives of the President abroad and are charged with representing Administration policies. Please select the answer that is closest to your opinion on who is more likely to be effective as ambassador at each of these goals.

Five goals were presented for respondents to identify which would be more effective for each goal: career ambassadors, appointed ambassadors, or equally effective. The results are presented in Figure 2.11.

Career ambassadors were consistently considered more effective than appointed ambassadors. Approximately 40 percent of respondents thought that career ambassadors were more effective at each goal, while roughly 35 percent of respondents believed that career and appointed ambassadors were equally effective at each goal. However, this was not because people tended to favor career ambassadors for all goals, or because respondents chose "equally effective" for all goals; only about one-quarter of respondents picked "career" for at least four of the five goals, and only about one-quarter picked "equally effective" for at least four of the five goals. In contrast, only 3 percent of respondents picked "appointed" for at least four of the five goals.

Men, respondents with college degrees, and those with higher incomes tended to consider career ambassadors to be more effective at most of the goals. Voters were also more likely to select career ambassadors for helping citizens abroad, and more-liberal respondents were more likely to select career ambassadors for reporting on developments abroad. Individuals who did not have a college degree or who were non-Hispanic black were more likely to favor appointed ambassadors' effectiveness over career ambassadors, or to consider both as equally effective, in each goal.

**FIGURE 2.11**
**Respondents' Perceived Efficacy of Career Versus Appointed Ambassadors, by Percentage, 2021**

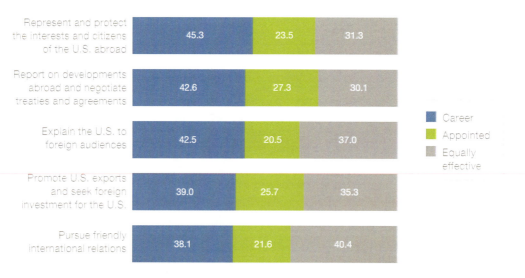

SOURCE: Analysis of RAND ALP data.
NOTE: Analysis includes survey weights. Percentages may not total 100 percent due to rounding.

# The Role of Diplomacy and the Foreign Service in National Security

Respondents were asked specifically about their view on the role of diplomacy with regard to national security (Figure 2.12). The majority of respondents agreed that "diplomacy contributes to our national security," although again a sizable minority reported "no opinion." Individuals who answered "yes" were more likely than others to be male, be non-Hispanic white, have a college degree, have higher income, and have voted in 2016.

Respondents were also asked whether they "think that diplomats or the military should lead U.S. efforts in most countries abroad." Figure 2.13 presents the responses in 2020 and again in 2021. Results were consistent over time, with the most common response being that diplomats, rather than the military, should lead. Next most common was "don't know/no opinion"; only about one-fifth of the respondents thought that the military should lead. Among those who expressed a preference, diplomats were the more likely choice for men, older respondents, non-Hispanic white respondents, those with a college degree, those with more-liberal political views, and those who voted in 2016.

**FIGURE 2.12**
**Perceptions of Whether Diplomacy Contributes to National Security, by Percentage, 2020–2021**

SOURCE: Analysis of RAND ALP data.
NOTE: Analysis includes survey weights.

**FIGURE 2.13**
**Perceptions of Whether Diplomats or the Military Should Lead Efforts Abroad, by Percentage, 2020–2021**

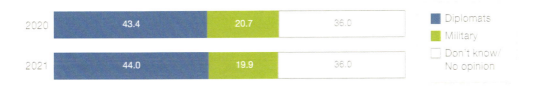

SOURCE: Analysis of RAND ALP data.
NOTE: Analysis includes survey weights.

# Perceptions of the Future of Diplomacy and the State Department

The majority of respondents continued to believe that "face-to-face diplomacy in order to represent that country and protect Americans in harm's way is effective and necessary in the digital age" (Figure 2.14). Men and respondents who were older, more highly educated, non-Hispanic white, and voters in 2016 were more likely to report that face-to-face diplomacy was still important. There was a significant decline in the proportion who responded "no opinion" in 2021 compared to 2020 (7 percentage points, a 28-percent drop in the overall size of the group), although the decline did not translate into a statistically significant increase in either of the other groups. Respondents who switched their opinion to "still important" in 2021 were more likely than others to be male, have high income, and be unmarried.

Respondents were asked to consider the funding that goes toward the State Department and American embassies. They were asked, "If you were making up the budget for the federal government next year, would you increase spending, decrease spending, or keep spending the same for the State Department and American Embassies?" This question has previously

### FIGURE 2.14
**Perceptions of Whether Face-to-Face Diplomacy Is Still Important in the Digital Age, by Percentage, 2020–2021**

SOURCE: Analysis of RAND ALP data.
NOTE: Analysis includes survey weights.

been asked by Pew in 2001, 2009, 2013, and 2017, allowing us to compare our survey data with existing time trends.[19] We asked this question in both the 2020 and 2021[20] surveys we fielded. Results from the Pew surveys as well as ours are presented in Figure 2.15. The 2020 and 2021 RAND results are generally consistent with the prior Pew findings, suggesting relative stability in perceptions over time. There were no changes in funding opinions among our survey respondents between 2020 and 2021, except for a non–statistically significant increase of 3 percentage points.

## Alternate Question Version in 2021

In the focus group discussions (described in the next chapter), it became clear that participants generally had no point of reference for what kind of funding the State Department currently receives, and many indicated that this prevented them from being able to form opinions. In response, for the second national ALP survey (2021), we modified the funding question for half the sample, so that while half received only the original (Pew) wording of the question, the other half of our sample received additional contextual information before the question on funding. These respondents with the alternate wording were informed that "Since 2010, about 1.2 percent–1.5 percent of the federal budget has gone to the State Department and American embassies. For comparison, about 15–20 percent of the federal budget has gone to the U.S. military during this time." Results for these respondents are presented in Figure 2.16. In comparison with the respondents who did not receive the additional information before being asked to answer the question, those who were given more context about the level of funding had a statistically significant 9-percentage-point increase in their "increase

---

[19] When making comparisons, note that the Pew sample includes adults ages 18 and older, while the ALP sample includes adults ages 24 and older. Pew also included "don't know/refused" options, while ALP respondents could skip the question but did not have an explicit "don't know" response option.

[20] In the 2021 survey, half of the sample received the original wording of the question. Only those respondents are included in Figure 2.15.

**FIGURE 2.15**

**Perceptions of the Adequacy of State Department Funding, by Percentage, 2001–2021**

Question: If you were making up the budget for the federal government next year, would you increase spending, decrease spending, or keep spending the same for the State Department and American embassies?

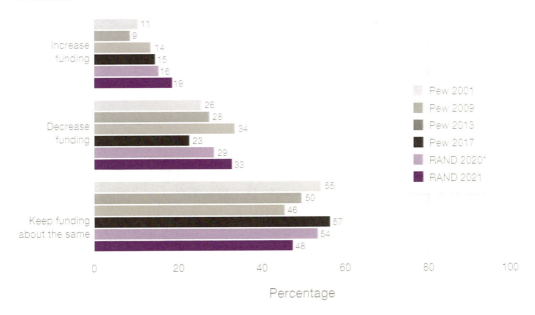

* RAND 2020 and 2021 results for this item are based on responses from half the sample, as described in the text.
SOURCES: Analysis of RAND ALP data. Pew surveys are Pew Research Center, 2001; Pew Research Center, 2009; Pew Research Center, 2013; and Pew Research Center, 2017.
NOTE: Analysis includes survey weights.

**FIGURE 2.16**

**Perceptions of the Adequacy of State Department Funding After Additional Information, by Percentage, 2020–2021**

Question: Since 2010, about 1.2 percent–1.5 percent of the federal budget has gone to the State Department and American embassies. For comparison, about 15–20 percent of the federal budget has gone to the U.S. military during this time. If you were making up the budget for the federal government next year, would you increase spending, decrease spending, or keep spending the same for the State Department and American embassies?

* RAND 2020 and 2021 results for this item are based on responses from half of the sample, as described in the text.
SOURCE: Analysis of RAND ALP data.
NOTE: Analysis includes survey weights.

funding" responses. This represents a 36-percent increase from baseline support for increasing State Department funding.

## Regional Differences in Attitudes

We explored the potential for regional differences in attitudes. First, we compared the proportions reporting either "very favorable" or "favorable" impressions of American diplomats and U.S. embassies abroad across the four main Census regions of the United States (identified in Figure 2.17) in 2020 and 2021 (Figure 2.18).

Most regions reported statistically equivalent levels of favorability to one another at both times. However, in 2020, favorable impressions were significantly higher in the West than they were in the Northeast or Midwest. In 2021, the only significant difference in favorability was between the Midwest (which was more favorable) and the Northeast. These differences were not completely diminished after sociodemographic and political variables were

**FIGURE 2.17**
**U.S. Census Regions**

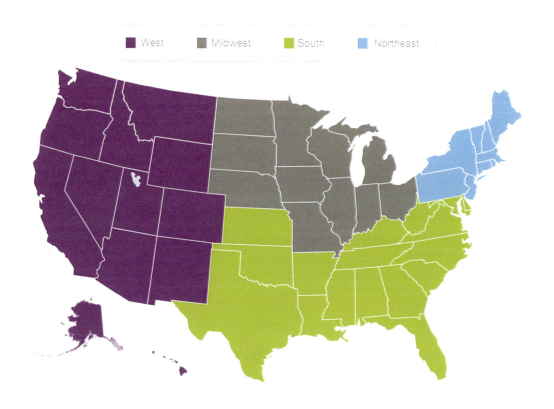

**FIGURE 2.18**
**Favorable Impressions of American Diplomats, by Census Region, 2020–2021**

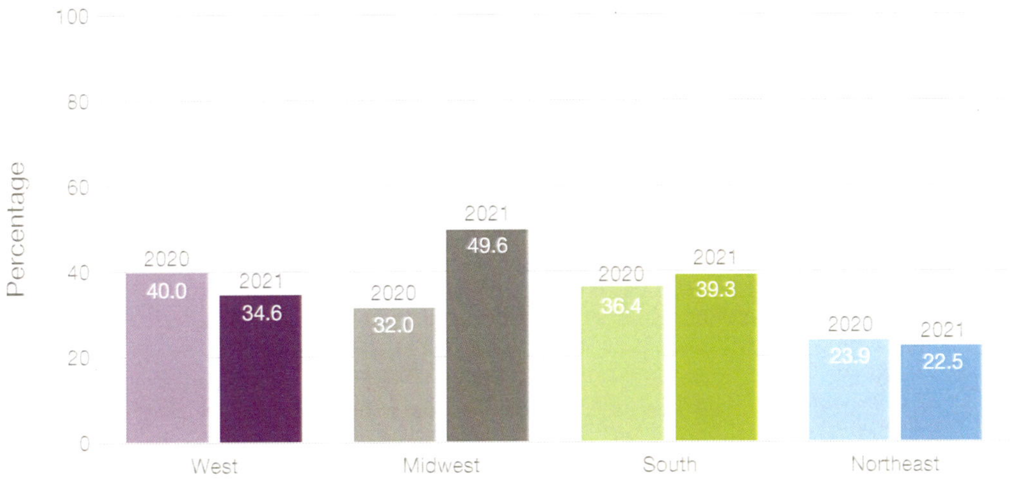

| Region | 2020 | 2021 |
|---|---|---|
| West | 40.0 | 34.6 |
| Midwest | 32.0 | 49.6 |
| South | 36.4 | 39.3 |
| Northeast | 23.9 | 22.5 |

SOURCE: Analysis of RAND ALP data.
NOTE: Analysis includes survey weights.

accounted for,[21] suggesting other underlying explanations for these attitudes. There were no significant regional differences in the proportions reporting "very favorable," "negative," or "very negative" impressions, meaning that any significant regional differences were due to differing levels of "favorable" and "neutral" impressions. Also note that changes in the level of favorability within regions did not change significantly over the year, complicating interpretation of the changing cross-regional differences (i.e., favorability in the Northeast and in the Midwest did not change significantly over time, but in 2020 they were equivalent to one another, and in 2021 they were significantly different from one another). Thus, regional differences in favorability should be interpreted with caution.

We also explored but did not identify regional differences in other attitudes, including confidence in the U.S. State Department; perceived importance of the Secretary of State or the State Department as a whole in determining the foreign policy of the United States; perceptions of diplomats as trustworthy, politically biased, or representative; whether diplomacy contributes to national security; support for State Department funding; diplomats leading efforts abroad compared to the military; and in the need for continued face-to-face diplomacy. As described in the next chapter, focus groups were conducted separately by region in an effort to explore potential regional differences, although regional patterns were not identified in the focus group analysis either.

---

[21] In a logistic regression model. See Appendix C, Table C.7.

## Added Questions on American Exceptionalism and American Values

As mentioned in Chapter Three, discussion arose organically in focus groups regarding participants' views of the Foreign Service in relation to American exceptionalism and American values. Thus, the research team decided to probe this further in the 2021 administration of the ALP with two additional questions.

One new item asked respondents about their belief in American exceptionalism using the question, "Some people say the United States has a unique character that makes it the greatest country in the world. Others say that every country is unique, and the United States is no greater than other nations. Which view is closer to your own?" More than half of the respondents, 62.5 percent, indicated a belief that the United States is the greatest country, while 37.5 percent responded that every country is unique. Respondents who agreed with American exceptionalism were more likely to be men, older, not have a college degree, and be more politically conservative. CCGA has surveyed this same question over time, noting a downward trend of 63 percent, 57 percent, and 54 percent of their sample stating that the United States was the greatest country in the world in 2017, 2019, and 2020, respectively.[22]

Another question added to the second ALP survey asked respondents about promoting American values around the world in order to be able to make broader interpretations of the comments that arose in the focus groups expressing concern about promoting such values: "In many periods of American history, our diplomats have promoted American values, as well as interests, abroad. Americans have believed that the United States would be more secure and more prosperous in a world in which our values such as democracy, freedom, human rights, and the rule of law were more widespread among other countries. How strongly do you agree or disagree with the statement: It is in America's interests to promote our values in today's world."

Figure 2.19 presents the distribution of responses. More than half of respondents agreed or strongly agreed, with less than 15 percent disagreeing. Older and higher-income individu-

**FIGURE 2.19**

**Perceptions of the Importance of Promoting American Values Through Diplomacy, by Percentage, 2021**

SOURCE: Analysis of RAND ALP data.
NOTE: Analysis includes survey weights.

---

[22] Smeltz et al., 2020.

als were more likely to agree, while there were no sociodemographic or political predictors of disagreement.

## Summary of Survey Results

Repeated surveys of a nationally representative sample of American residents indicated that the State Department is among a cluster of institutions (along with the White House, the military, and intelligence organizations) that the public views with relatively high and (recently) increasing confidence to shape policies that benefit the United States. The State Department receives broad support from the public, with no significant differences by sociodemographic or political factors apart from age (confidence was higher among older individuals). Perceptions of the importance of both the State Department and the Secretary of State in determining foreign policy were similarly high, and stable overall. While the Secretary of State is viewed with equal importance across the political spectrum, the importance of the State Department more broadly was linked to political ideology (more-liberal individuals increased their perception of the State Department's importance between 2020 and 2021).

In general, respondents did not have a high level of knowledge about the Foreign Service or U.S. diplomats, and many expressed a lack of opinion on a wide range of related topics. Respondents who reported lower levels of knowledge about the Foreign Service were more likely than those with higher levels of knowledge to respond "no opinion" to subsequent questions. Furthermore, those with lower levels of knowledge were more likely to provide responses that were less favorable toward the Foreign Service or diplomats. However, expressed opinions overall tended to be favorable or neutral toward the Foreign Service, with explicitly negative opinions representing a small minority. Broadly, American diplomats tended to be viewed as "trustworthy" but "politically biased." Between 2020 and 2021, respondents were somewhat more likely to consider diplomats to not be representative of the American population.

Generally, respondents with higher educational attainment, men, those who voted in the 2016 presidential election, those with higher incomes, and those who were older held more-positive views about the Foreign Service and American diplomats than others. Political views were generally not linked to perceptions of overall favorability or confidence in the State Department, but they were linked to perceptions about the types of characteristics that diplomats should have and the tasks that they perform.

Respondents indicated that the most important function of diplomats is helping American citizens while abroad. Perceptions of other important functions varied by socioeconomic status, with higher-socioeconomic-status respondents viewing diplomats as having proactive global outreach roles, and lower-socioeconomic-status individuals viewing diplomats as having important defensive or protective functions. Those with more-liberal political views prioritized global activities, such as promoting cooperation against global threats and understanding global affairs, while those with more-conservative views prioritized domestic politics, fighting terrorism, and policy discipline.

Survey respondents indicated support for the State Department taking a leading role in making foreign policy and a belief that diplomacy contributed to national security. There was a broad perception that diplomacy was still important in the digital age. Most respondents supported keeping the level of funding for the State Department the same in the future, although providing context on the relative level of funding it receives increased the likelihood that respondents would support an increased budget in the future.

In the next chapter, we expand on these survey findings through a series of focus group discussions exploring opinions on the Foreign Service and the State Department, helping increase our understanding as to why members of the public hold the views that they have on diplomacy and diplomats.

CHAPTER THREE

# Findings from In-Depth Focus Group Discussions

To better understand why Americans hold the views identified in the ALP survey, RAND researchers led a series of in-depth focus groups around the United States with a group of participants separate from the ALP. The goal of the focus groups was to complement and provide context for the results of the survey analyses. The focus group interviews are not intended to be generalizable to the public overall but rather are used to explore and illustrate the diverse ways people talk and think about the types of questions we asked in the surveys. In addition, novel topics of discussion emerged, as did several overall themes related to how the focus groups perceived the Foreign Service and American diplomats.

The original research design was to hold eight in-person focus groups in four cities around the country. Due to the coronavirus pandemic, however, all groups were conducted virtually on either Microsoft Teams or Zoom, using both audio and video. Two advantages of virtual sessions were that they allowed a wide geographical reach within the four Census-defined regions that we were examining (Northeast, South, Midwest, and West), and, since no researcher travel was required, they allowed more focus groups to be conducted within a tighter time frame. In all, RAND researchers led 14 focus groups between December 2020 and March 2021, with a total of 118 individuals in attendance.

We used a trusted external vendor to recruit individuals to participate in the focus groups. The vendor has locations in 13 metro areas around the United States and maintains databases of individuals in each area who have previously agreed to be contacted about participating in studies. We specified search parameters, requesting diversity by age, geography, gender, education, race/ethnicity, political affiliation, possession of a passport, and familiarity with the U.S. Foreign Service. Individuals were ineligible to participate if they indicated that they were "not at all familiar" with U.S. Foreign Service and American diplomats. Individuals were offered a $100 payment for participation in the focus groups.

We provided a screening script that was used to collect demographic and other information needed to ensure that diversity in each of the parameters was reached. The vendor contacted members of their database and verified the responses to each of the screening questions. Table 3.1 provides a breakdown of participant characteristics.

Focus groups were stratified by geography so that all individuals in each group were located in one geographic region (Northeast, South, Midwest, or West). We conducted three

**TABLE 3.1**
**Focus Group Characteristics**

|  | n = 118 | Percentage |
|---|---|---|
| Gender | | |
|     Male | 59 | 50% |
|     Female | 59 | 50% |
| Race/ethnicity | | |
|     White non-Hispanic | 65 | 55% |
|     Black/African American | 23 | 19% |
|     Hispanic/Latino | 23 | 19% |
|     Asian | 6 | 5% |
|     Other | 1 | 1% |
| Age | | |
|     21–35 | 42 | 36% |
|     36–50 | 38 | 32% |
|     51–65 | 31 | 26% |
|     66+ | 7 | 6% |
| Education | | |
|     High school graduate or GED (General Educational Development test) | 3 | 3% |
|     Some college or two-year degree | 32 | 27% |
|     Four-year college graduate | 48 | 41% |
|     More than four-year college degree | 35 | 30% |
| Region | | |
|     Northeast | 37 | 31% |
|     Midwest | 23 | 20% |
|     South | 26 | 22% |
|     West | 32 | 27% |
| Political views | | |
|     Liberal or very liberal | 43 | 36% |
|     Moderate | 40 | 34% |
|     Conservative or very conservative | 35 | 30% |
| Familiarity with Foreign Service | | |
|     Not too familiar | 44 | 37% |
|     Somewhat familiar | 65 | 55% |
|     Very familiar | 9 | 8% |

groups with participants from the Midwest, four with participants from the Northeast, three from the South, and four from the West. Additionally, groups in each region were stratified by education, with five high-education groups (in which all participants had a bachelor's degree or higher), two lower-education groups (in which all participants had less than a bachelor's degree), and seven mixed-education groups.[1] For the initial groups, we recruited 11 participants per group, later revising our procedures to recruit nine participants per group. Because some groups had last-minute cancellations, each group had between six and 11 attendees.

A member of the RAND team met with each recruited individual in advance of the focus group to confirm their participation and ensure that they had access to the correct meeting software, as well as audio and video capability. During these meetings, participants were provided with instruction on the software, including how to display only their first names during the group, how to mute and unmute themselves, and how to turn on their video. They were reminded to sit in a private, quiet space during the focus group and to sign in 15 minutes early to ensure that their equipment was working correctly. At the start of each focus group, an instruction slide was displayed to remind participants how to use the software. RAND staff were present to assist participants who were having difficulty joining the session or with the software features.

Each focus group was approximately 90 minutes long and followed a structured protocol (Appendix D). Groups were led by a member of RAND's Survey Research Group[2] staff experienced in focus group moderation, and project research staff observed all focus groups. The focus group began with an introduction that covered the purpose of the group, noted the funder, gave assurances of confidentiality, and provided rules to ensure that the group would run smoothly with maximum participation. The focus group protocol covered topics such as impressions of diplomacy and diplomats, embassy functions, choosing diplomats and concerns for their safety, and the future of diplomacy. Participants were also asked about their own experience with embassies or diplomats. Exhibits were used to explain concepts, provide examples or talking points for participants to react to, and steer conversation onto new topic areas. Moderators called on participants as needed to ensure participation by everyone in each group. Each focus group was recorded and transcribed, and the nearly 600 pages of deidentified verbatim transcripts were used for analysis.

Except during the discussion segment targeted at criteria for the selection of career FSOs, focus group facilitators used terms like "American diplomats" or "American diplomacy" rather than the less widely understood terms "FSOs" or "Foreign Service."

---

[1] Groups were stratified to encourage similar levels of engagement in discussion by participants with different levels of educational attainment. In the early focus group sessions, we observed less participation from focus group members with lower levels of educational attainment when the majority of the group was of substantially higher education. High- and mixed-education groups were held in all regions. Two low-education groups were held in the Northeast and the West.

[2] The Survey Research Group provides RAND with in-house capability for conducting primary data collection and is composed of methodologists and specialists in the operational and technical aspects of survey and qualitative data collection.

Focus group topics largely replicated the ALP survey content, with the goal of eliciting discussions around topics that supplemented the survey findings. Each member of the research team carefully reviewed the transcripts and initially developed a list of common findings from each group under each discussion topic, which were then aggregated to generate a short list of key findings across groups, as well as broader themes that emerged in the focus groups beyond the explicit answers to questions themselves. Findings and broader themes identified by each research team member were then compared and discussed by the rest of the team. The key findings and broader themes presented below are all those independently identified by two or more of the team members. Illustrative quotes supporting results and themes are also provided. Results are intended to provide supplemental context to the ALP results with illustrative examples and are not intended to be generalizable. Statements of relative frequencies are intended to convey a sense of prevalence and diversity where distinct differences were noted by team members. Below, we summarize the identified themes and provide illustrative quotes reflecting the findings.

## Associations with the Term *American Diplomacy*

After ice-breaking questions,[3] the facilitator asked the groups the following question: "When you hear the term *American diplomacy*, what comes to mind?" This question yielded a wide variety of responses. Some participants thought of diplomatic *functions*, like "eyes and ears abroad"[4] and "building connections and rapport with foreign countries,"[5] or people who help Americans facing difficulties, such as lost passports. Others thought of *goals*, such as soothing tensions and mediating disputes,[6] advancing trade interests,[7] promoting economic policies,[8] or keeping the United States out of war, which was one of the most common and immediate responses.[9] For example, one participant stated that "American diplomacy [is] the alternative to armed conflict,"[10] while another said, "We won't have peace if we don't get to

---

[3] "What single word describes you?" and "How closely do you follow the news?"

[4] Focus group 6, West, February 11, 2021, transcript, p. 6.

[5] Focus group 9, Midwest, March 11, 2021, transcript, p. 6.

[6] E.g., focus group 3, Northeast, February 2, 2021, transcript, p. 8; focus group 4, Midwest, February 4, 2021, transcript, p. 5; focus group 10, Midwest, March 15, 2021, transcript, p. 6.

[7] E.g., focus group 1, Northeast, December 14, 2020, transcript, p. 4.

[8] E.g., focus group 1, Northeast, December 14, 2020, transcript, p. 5; focus group 5, South, February 9, 2021, transcript, p. 7.

[9] E.g., focus group 1, Northeast, December 14, 2020, transcript, p. 5; focus group 4, Midwest, February 4, 2021, transcript, p. 30; focus group 5, South, February 9, 2021, transcript, p. 7.

[10] Focus group 11, South, March 17, 2021, transcript, p. 8.

know each other, if we don't have relationships with each other."[11] One participant described diplomacy as "finding that win-win for everybody,"[12] and another participant expressed that diplomacy "is about talking" and dialogue.[13] Across the groups, strong emphasis was put on relationship-building, maintenance, and management as necessary; one participant called this "the biggest need"[14] even if it does not have immediate returns. Similarly, participants across most focus groups expressed that diplomacy is essential for "national security."

In some groups, participants also described American diplomacy as helping other countries, in terms of improving human rights around the world,[15] disaster recovery,[16] or other types of aid.[17] These participants mentioned that we should not be looking to diplomacy for immediate gains for the United States but rather should be thinking about the benefits of relationships down the road and that "mature leadership" would view diplomacy in terms of aid and relationship-building.[18]

These general responses previewed the range of responses that would follow more-specific questions later in the sessions.

On the positive side, even unprompted, many respondents generally thought that having American diplomats on the ground in countries around the world was important for the protection of American citizens (the most-mentioned specific advantages of diplomats),[19] for obtaining good relations with other countries,[20] as an alternative to armed conflict,[21] for serving as U.S. "eyes and ears,"[22] for acting as "negotiators" or "mediators" of disputes, and for promoting U.S. culture. One participant observed that diplomacy "costs less than missiles."[23]

On the negative side, some of the participants' first responses cited political appointees (and presidential donors) appointed as ambassadors overseas in terms of "political payoffs,"[24]

---

[11] Focus group 4, Midwest, February 4, 2021, transcript, p. 30.

[12] Focus group 12, West, March 23, 2021, transcript, p. 8.

[13] Focus group 12, West, March 23, 2021, transcript, p. 11.

[14] Focus group 12, West, March 23, 2021, transcript, p. 8.

[15] E.g., focus group 8, South, March 9, 2021, transcript, p. 9.

[16] E.g., focus group 11, South, March 17, 2021, transcript, p. 9.

[17] E.g., focus group 3, Northeast, February 2, 2021, transcript, p. 7; focus group 11, South, March 17, 2021, transcript, p. 26.

[18] E.g., focus group 12, West, March 23, 2021, transcript, p. 7.

[19] E.g., focus group 9, Midwest, March 11, 2021, transcript, p. 6.

[20] E.g., focus group 11, South, March 17, 2021, transcript, p. 7.

[21] E.g., focus group 11, South, March 17, 2021, transcript, p. 8.

[22] Focus group 6, West, February 11, 2021, transcript, p. 6.

[23] Focus group 1, Northeast, December 14, 2020, transcript, p. 9.

[24] Focus group 6, West, February 11, 2021, transcript, p. 6.

said that American diplomacy was being "overrun by the Chinese,"[25] or more commonly admitted that they did not hear or know much about American diplomacy because it was not covered much by the media.[26] One participant considered diplomacy to be a "tax-paid vacation" without "much coming out."[27] A few participants introduced American domestic politics in their answers, noting that the role of diplomacy depended on who was in the White House[28] or recalling that, in the 2019 impeachment process, diplomats were "thrown under the bus"[29] and "treated shabbily."[30]

## Perceptions of the Success of American Diplomacy

The first specific topic for the groups was to discuss whether they considered American diplomacy to be broadly successful or unsuccessful. Success was assessed by a wide range of measures throughout the groups. For example, some participants considered lack of new wars or conflicts a "success"[31] or thought that the fact that little is heard about diplomacy was a measure of success.[32] There were a number of observations that American diplomacy must be successful, because the public "doesn't hear about it" or only hears about the few situations that "don't turn out well," with Benghazi being commonly given as an example.[33]

Some participants also brought in their domestic political perspectives in making such value judgments, expressing the opinion that former President Trump ruined relationships with allies,[34] noting that public opinion of the United States in 13 major countries averages only 34 percent,[35] or suggesting that presidents get to determine foreign policy because "elec-

---

[25] Focus group 10, Midwest, March 15, 2021, transcript, p. 7.

[26] E.g., focus group 1, Northeast, December 14, 2020, transcript, p. 8; focus group 6, West, February 11, 2021, transcript, p. 15; focus group 7, West, March 4, 2021, transcript, p. 9.

[27] Focus group 8, South, March 9, 2021, transcript, p. 7.

[28] Focus group 14, Northeast, March 30, 2021, transcript, p. 8.

[29] Focus group 14, Northeast, March 30, 2021, transcript, p. 9.

[30] Focus group 14, Northeast, March 30, 2021, transcript, p. 22.

[31] E.g., focus group 1, Northeast, December 14, 2020, transcript, p. 8; focus group 11, South, March 17, 2021, transcript, p. 12; focus group 13, West, March 25, 2021, transcript, p. 13.

[32] E.g., focus group 4, Midwest, February 4, 2021, transcript, p. 13; focus group 13, West, March 25, 2021, transcript, p. 17.

[33] E.g., focus group 11, South, March 17, 2021, transcript, p. 17.

[34] E.g., focus group 11, South, March 17, 2021, transcript, p. 14; focus group 12, West, March 23, 2021, transcript, p. 6; focus group 14, Northeast, March 30, 2021, transcript, p. 14.

[35] Focus group 12, West, March 23, 2021, transcript, p. 17.

tions have consequences."[36] One participant viewed American diplomacy as bullying behavior, as in "we're going to tell you what [we] want and then we're going to take it."[37]

Another way success was measured was by the quality of relationships with other countries, which varied depending on the country.[38] One participant described American diplomacy as 80 to 90 percent successful but noted that the one exception was policy related to "the Middle East," where, in terms of security and humanitarian needs, the participant said that the United States had not succeeded at all.[39] Another participant opined that diplomats focus on very short-term economic benefits rather than long-term relationships, so that in terms of "American economic interest," diplomacy has been successful.[40]

Conversely, a source of failure of American diplomacy was identified by one participant as not knowing "our" objectives with which to shape diplomacy because there is no unified "our."[41] This participant pointed to domestic challenges facing diversity and inclusion as negatively impacting American diplomacy. Other factors that negatively impact American diplomacy were discussed, such as public lack of interest in world affairs and an educational system that has led Americans to believe that they are superior to people in other countries.

## Perceptions of Appropriate Goals of American Diplomacy

Digging deeper into what focus groups thought of diplomacy, facilitators asked what participants thought the goals of American diplomacy should be. A variety of different observations emerged. Some responses for the main goal of diplomacy were peace,[42] managing relationships with other countries,[43] avoiding nuclear war,[44] and promoting business.[45]

---

[36] Focus group 6, West, February 11, 2021, transcript, p. 18.

[37] Focus group 7, West, March 4, 2021, transcript, p. 10.

[38] E.g., focus group 1, Northeast, December 14, 2020, transcript, p. 8; focus group 7, West, March 4, 2021, transcript, p. 14; focus group 11, South, March 17, 2021, transcript, p. 13.

[39] Focus group 13, West, March 25, 2021, transcript, p. 14.

[40] Focus group 13, West, March 25, 2021, transcript, p. 16.

[41] Focus group 12, West, March 23, 2021, transcript, p. 16.

[42] E.g., focus group 2, Northeast, December 17, 2020, transcript, p. 5; focus group 10, Midwest, March 15, 2021, transcript, p. 8.

[43] E.g., focus group 12, West, March 23, 2021, transcript, p. 7.

[44] E.g., focus group 14, Northeast, March 30, 2021, transcript, p. 15.

[45] E.g., focus group 6, West, February 11, 2021, transcript, p. 11; focus group 10, Midwest, March 15, 2021, transcript, p. 8.

More-mundane tasks that were mentioned included "representation, necessary even when there are differences,"[46] staying informed,[47] keeping criminals from traveling,[48] and preparing summits and other meetings.[49] One participant mentioned promotion of human rights,[50] and another said that efforts to attract foreign students to U.S. institutions were driven by an interest in attracting full-tuition payers.[51]

## Importance of Tasks of American Diplomats

In testing the focus group protocol, the research team found that the discussions could be usefully supplemented after the free-association sections by displaying on a screen a list of illustrative tasks that diplomats perform. We used the list of generic functions shown below to stimulate discussion, asking participants whether they found any of these tasks surprising and to discuss which functions were most and least important.

- protecting American citizens in trouble
- representing U.S. policy to foreign governments and publics
- promoting American exports from U.S. farms and manufacturers
- deciding on visa applications from foreigners seeking to visit the United States
- reporting on developments in foreign countries
- promoting and explaining U.S. values
- engaging foreign publics to inform and influence them about U.S. values and policy priorities to enhance the U.S. international image or generate a more favorable view of the United States abroad
- informing U.S. foreign policy by providing actionable feedback to the National Security Council and the executive branch.

Almost universally, participants across the groups identified the first task—protecting Americans in trouble—as the most important function.[52] A number of participants had first- or second-hand stories to relate, when travelers they knew were robbed or lost passports, and embassy or consulate officers efficiently and promptly arranged new documentation. One of several participants who initially equated American diplomacy with protecting travelers

---

[46] Focus group 9, Midwest, March 11, 2021, transcript, p. 11.

[47] Focus group 7, West, March 4, 2021, transcript, p. 9.

[48] Focus group 7, West, March 4, 2021, transcript, p. 11.

[49] Focus group 10, Midwest, March 15, 2021, transcript, p. 12.

[50] Focus group 8, South, March 9, 2021, transcript, p. 9.

[51] Focus group 14, Northeast, March 30, 2021, transcript, p. 11.

[52] E.g., focus group 3, Northeast, February 2, 2021, transcript, p. 7; focus group 8, South, March 9, 2021, transcript, p. 11; focus group 14, Northeast, March 30, 2021, transcript, p. 29.

viewed diplomats' roles as a service "so we feel like when we're somewhere else, we're not alone and we do have somewhere to go with any questions or any problems that come up."[53]

The task next most commonly cited as most important was reporting on developments in foreign countries[54]—which, for example, participants considered important for determining what was "really" going on abroad, even (or especially) in an era of information overload (also see the section "The Future of American Diplomacy" later in this chapter). One participant called this function a source of "raw information" about what's happening abroad.[55]

When participants were asked whether they were "surprised" by any of the tasks presented on the list, two tasks were cited as surprising more than any other: promoting exports[56] and deciding on visa applications.

Among those who had not previously known that American diplomats have a role in export promotion among their responsibilities, participants seemed divided about whether the task should be undertaken by FSOs. Some participants were sympathetic to export promotion,[57] while others either did not think that diplomats could do it well[58] or thought that it would inappropriately benefit private business. One participant said,

> I knew that [promoting exports] was probably something that happened by nature of having a large group of probably Americans living and working in a concentrated area.... But I didn't know that was something we were doing on purpose. But I guess it's good.[59]

Another participant was more skeptical of the appropriateness, stating that it "looks more like a business interest . . . that's more like a trade group."[60]

Making decisions on visa applications, while a surprise to some participants, did not seem to raise as many questions of appropriateness one way or another. For example, one participant stated, "I didn't know they did that. I didn't think that actually went through the Foreign Service. Do they do that for everybody?"[61]

---

[53] Focus group 2, Northeast, December 17, 2020, transcript, p. 13.

[54] E.g., focus group 9, Midwest, March 11, 2021, transcript, p. 30; focus group 12, West, March 23, 2021, transcript, p. 29; focus group 14, Northeast, March 30, 2021, transcript, p. 28.

[55] Focus group 10, Midwest, March 15, 2021, transcript, p. 14.

[56] E.g., focus group 5, South, February 9, 2021, transcript, p. 16; focus group 11, South, March 17, 2021, transcript, p. 25.

[57] E.g., focus group 7, West, March 4, 2021, transcript, p. 25.

[58] Focus group 8, South, March 9, 2021, transcript, p. 29.

[59] Focus group 3, Northeast, February 2, 2021, transcript, p. 20.

[60] Focus group 10, Midwest, March 15, 2021, transcript, p. 21.

[61] Focus group 6, West, February 11, 2021, transcript, p. 27.

The diplomatic task that stimulated the most reaction across the groups was engaging foreign publics to inform and influence them about U.S. values and policy priorities.[62] Many participants were critical of this task, considering in particular that the "values" and policy priorities that might be promoted would change between administrations[63] or might be considered "preaching,"[64] "bullying or sticking our nose in somebody else's business,"[65] "imposing our way of thinking"[66] with ideas "that are not always welcome in other countries,"[67] or culturally biased ("who's to say that some of their values are not as important as ours?").[68] In some cases, such concerns were explicitly related to domestic political polarization: "I think the two sides might disagree on what the values that are promoted should be."[69] Several participants indicated a belief that polarization had further impacts, with one noting, "[t]he divisiveness between the Democrats and the Republicans here in the States I think gives a confusing message to the world."[70] When this subject arose in one of the early focus groups, one of the participants expressed skepticism about values promotion, noting that *values* was "such a loaded word." The full exchange appears below, illustrating that for some of the participants, promotion of an American value even as basic as "democracy" could be risky.

> Participant 1: I just feel like *values* is such a loaded word, and I think [Participant 3] was talking about it earlier how we believe in certain inalienable rights that we have as humans and trying to pose that on other people or not or go against people who disagree with it. So, I feel like who gets to choose what the U.S. values are. I don't know. I guess I would need an example of what a U.S. value is that they would be promoting because I can't even think of one that we don't have division on within ourselves.
>
> Participant 2: Gay rights.
>
> Moderator: Okay. So, it sounds like they agree. So, people are kind of surprised by this thing about values because it's something that can change depending on the administra-

---

[62] In the 2021 CCGA survey, respondents also placed "promoting democracy and human rights around the world," "taking leadership in international issues," and "participating in international organizations" relatively low on the list of factors important to the United States "remaining influential in the world" (Smeltz et al., 2021, p. 4).

[63] E.g., focus group 3, Northeast, February 2, 2021, transcript, p. 35; focus group 5, South, February 9, 2021, transcript, p. 12 focus group 7, West, March 4, 2021, transcript, p. 10; focus group 10, Midwest, March 15, 2021, transcript, p. 28.

[64] Focus group 11, South, March 17, 2021, transcript, p. 29.

[65] Focus group 3, Northeast, February 2, 2021, transcript, p. 23.

[66] Focus group 3, Northeast, February 2, 2021, transcript, p. 23.

[67] Focus group 5, South, February 9, 2021, transcript, p. 12.

[68] Focus group 14, Northeast, March 30, 2021, transcript, p. 31.

[69] Focus group 4, Midwest, February 4, 2021, transcript, p. 23.

[70] Focus group 10, Midwest, March 15, 2021, transcript, p. 22.

tion. It's not necessarily something that all people would necessarily agree on one way or the other. Is that what I'm hearing you say?

Participant 1: Yeah.

Moderator: Okay. And what about some other people who we haven't heard from yet? And actually, I have in the chat here a message from [RAND researcher observer]. And he made the point that an example of a U.S. value that would be promoted is something like *democracy*. So, the point being that it's not necessarily the type of value that is a big social issue, but it could be something that hopefully we all agree on as a U.S. value.

Participant 3: But isn't it true that we do have controversial policies and views that we try to push on other countries? And without making a judgment on one, I know that we financially either punish or incentivize countries based on how they implement what we view as abortion rights. So, I'm sure there are other examples.[71]

## Additional ALP Questions on Perceptions of America

Discussion and concern around American values was consistently robust across focus groups. In response to how commonly these issues arose, as noted in Chapter Two, we added two items to the second ALP survey to assess the extent of related attitudes at the population level through generalizable analysis.

## Selection and Characteristics of Foreign Service Officers

For the focus group discussion of characteristics and selection of FSOs, as with the previous discussion of "tasks," the research team posted the following illustrative list of selection criteria on participants' screens:

- language fluency
- understanding global affairs
- bravery in the face of danger
- negotiating skill
- public speaking
- diversity.

The moderator explained that FSOs were selected by an examination process. Participants were asked which of the listed criteria were considered by the group to be most important and least important and whether any were missing.

---

[71] Focus group 5, South, February 9, 2021, transcript, pp. 18–19.

While only a few participants said that they personally knew any FSOs, this segment generated robust discussion for most of the groups. Many said that their general opinion of career American diplomats was "positive,"[72] for a variety of reasons, explaining, for example, "they're sacrificing a lot for us,"[73] "[t]hey really are putting themselves in a place where there really is no guarantee . . . [t]hey are very dedicated and because of their risk in going overseas to protect us, I feel that I'm indebted to them,"[74] or "these are people who probably have very clean records and know multiple languages and have studies where they're going to be . . . They're probably the cream of the crop."[75] Some stated that they had no opinion because they hadn't met any diplomats,[76] or because they simply did not know enough to say.[77]

Across the groups, each criterion shown on screen was discussed by participants as being important, but language fluency tended to emerge as one of the most important.[78] The importance of language fluency was commonly justified because it improved the ability to negotiate effectively.[79] One participant noted a specific difficulty of vetting interpreters as a reason that language fluency was especially important.[80]

Some disagreement emerged in discussion of the last criterion listed, diversity. Diversity was not formally defined for participants, and while it could be interpreted in different ways, it was primarily discussed in terms of racial and ethnic diversity. Some participants questioned it, thinking that only exam outcomes should be relevant for selection[81] or asking whether the ethnic background of diplomats sent to specific countries mattered, since "we're all Americans."[82] But other participants also saw the value of a diverse Foreign Service since it would give diplomats more cultural sensitivity and awareness of differences, which is valuable for effective service abroad.[83] A diverse Foreign Service also offers more potential to

---

[72] E.g., focus group 3, Northeast, February 2, 2021, transcript, p. 25; focus group 12, West, March 23, 2021, transcript, p. 36; focus group 13, West, March 25, 2021, transcript, p. 33.

[73] Focus group 4, Midwest, February 4, 2021, transcript, p. 28.

[74] Focus group 7, West, March 4, 2021, transcript, p. 30.

[75] Focus group 10, Midwest, March 15, 2021, transcript, p. 30.

[76] Focus group 11, South, March 17, 2021, transcript, p. 31.

[77] E.g., focus group 7, West, March 4, 2021, transcript, p. 51; focus group 8, South, March 9, 2021, transcript, p. 35.

[78] E.g., focus group 7, West, March 4, 2021, transcript, p. 46; focus group 9, Midwest, March 11, 2021, transcript, p. 38.

[79] Focus group 3, Northeast, February 2, 2021, transcript, p. 45.

[80] Focus group 7, West, March 4, 2021, transcript, p. 46.

[81] E.g., focus group 2, Northeast, December 17, 2020, transcript, p. 22.

[82] Focus group 12, West, March 23, 2021, transcript, p. 48.

[83] E.g., focus group 9, Midwest, March 11, 2021, transcript, p. 41; focus group 10, Midwest, March 15, 2021, transcript, p. 44; focus group 12, West, March 23, 2021, transcript, p. 47; focus group 13, West, March 25, 2021, transcript, p. 49.

match the characteristics of the local population in foreign postings, to enhance the sense of American diversity or to facilitate connection, as described by one participant:

> Well, I think that especially there are a lot of countries where the population culturally and racially doesn't match what we have in the U.S. and that if you were to send, let's just say, white Catholics into a black Islam country or whatever, I think it sends the message that we're not very culturally sensitive. The U.S. is made up of a lot of people and I think we need to utilize that *diversity* to further understanding and to make these skills more useful.[84]

Participants were also asked what additional criteria should be important in the selection of diplomats. Many additional criteria were proposed, thereby illuminating what participants considered valuable characteristics in diplomats: communication skills,[85] leadership and management skills,[86] cultural awareness,[87] ethics,[88] honesty,[89] empathy,[90] knowing how government works,[91] and being tech savvy.[92]

In this segment, focus group participants also were asked whether there would be value in having American diplomats spend time in U.S. communities outside of Washington. Again, participants expressed differing views. Participants who said that there would be value in such exposure[93] noted that, in addition to potentially helping the public understand what diplomats do, diplomats would thereby be able to better understand subcultures in America,[94] learn about domestic problems relevant to foreign affairs,[95] or understand who Americans

---

[84] Focus group 11, South, March 17, 2021, transcript, p. 48.

[85] Focus group 10, Midwest, March 15, 2021, transcript, p. 45.

[86] Focus group 11, South, March 17, 2021, transcript, p. 45.

[87] Focus group 6, West, February 11, 2021, transcript, p. 44; focus group 7, West, March 4, 2021, transcript, p. 45; focus group 8, South, March 9, 2021, transcript, p. 43; focus group 9, Midwest, March 11, 2021, transcript, p. 43.

[88] Focus group 7, West, March 4, 2021, transcript, p. 43.

[89] Focus group 11, South, March 17, 2021, transcript, p. 48; focus group 14, Northeast, March 30, 2021, transcript, p. 44.

[90] Focus group 4, Midwest, February 4, 2021, transcript, p. 37; focus group 5, South, February 9, 2021, transcript, p. 39; focus group 10, Midwest, March 15, 2021, transcript, p. 41.

[91] Focus group 6, West, February 11, 2021, transcript, p. 44.

[92] Focus group 2, Northeast, December 17, 2020, transcript, p. 17; focus group 9, Midwest, March 11, 2021, transcript, p. 38.

[93] E.g., focus group 12, West, March 23, 2021, transcript, p. 42; focus group 14, Northeast, March 30, 2021, transcript, p. 43.

[94] Focus group 11, South, March 17, 2021, transcript, p. 39.

[95] Focus group 11, South, March 17, 2021, transcript, p. 42.

really are.[96] In contrast, some participants questioned the "vague purpose" of the idea[97] or said that time spent in Washington between assignments abroad should be sufficient to sensitize FSOs to domestic concerns.[98]

## The Future of American Diplomacy

The final segment of the focus group sessions elicited participants' views of the future of American diplomacy, its relationship to the military, its place in U.S. government decision-making, and how much the nation should spend on its diplomatic establishment.

The general consensus across groups was that diplomacy would be more important in the future. Participants commonly observed that the "world is getting smaller" from globalization and technology and that there would be a growing need for active diplomacy to protect the nation's interests,[99] such as the participant who stated:

> [Diplomacy is] definitely going to be more important because the world is shrinking now. I know physically not shrinking, but it's shrinking in terms of the availability of information and travel and things like that. So as more and more people bump up against each other, it's going to be more important to be able to work out our differences and to understand each other for the betterment of humankind.[100]

On the subject of technology, one participant commented that technology can send an "unmanned drone" to gather intelligence but could "not [be used] to build relationships."[101] The notion that in-person diplomacy would continue to be important despite innovations in communications technology was explicitly supported in every group, with one participant commenting, "It's the same in business, you've got to have salesmen go out and build relationships to get sales. . . . We've got to have somebody over there making those kinds of relationships that count."[102]

---

[96] Focus group 6, West, February 11, 2021, transcript, p. 43.

[97] Focus group 11, South, March 17, 2021, transcript, p. 40.

[98] Focus group 12, West, March 23, 2021, transcript, p. 44.

[99] E.g., focus group 4, Midwest, February 4, 2021, transcript, p. 39; focus group 6, West, February 11, 2021, transcript, p. 49; focus group 8, South, March 9, 2021, transcript, p. 48; focus group 9, Midwest, March 11, 2021, transcript, p. 45; focus group 11, South, March 17, 2021, transcript, p. 50.

[100] Focus group 13, West, March 25, 2021, transcript, p. 50.

[101] Focus group 9, Midwest, March 11, 2021, transcript, p. 48.

[102] Focus group 10, Midwest, March 15, 2021, transcript, p. 33.

Others commented that we need diplomacy to be able to negotiate through and avoid armed conflict[103] or solve global problems together,[104] such as climate change[105] and pandemics.[106] Across the groups, there was also a general sense of increasing global volatility that would require increased diplomatic efforts to counter.[107] For example, one participant said, "the world is becoming more complex, more and more dangerous . . . people are becoming less and less patient and tolerant of the stress."[108] Another stated that we are "living in a world where tensions can arise much higher and quicker. . . . Information can get spread very quickly. And I think we need more people to help negotiate and help keep things real. And we need boots on the ground."[109] In this context, diplomats in foreign countries were envisioned as an "advanced notice" system for conflicts, so that "we could know that it's coming and we could prepare for it . . . You just never want to wake up to [it]—that's almost like an earthquake."[110]

Participants were asked whether diplomats or the military should lead efforts in most countries abroad. As in the nationwide ALP survey, most, though not all, focus group participants considered it better for diplomats to lead, on the grounds such as that diplomats "promote peace"[111] or that other countries tend to see the U.S. military as "aggressive."[112] No participants considered it best for the military to lead in all cases, though some suggested that it depended on the situation on the ground. One participant said, "you don't want a diplomat in there trying to talk to ISIS [the Islamic State of Iraq and Syria] and telling them 'stand down' because they won't do it."[113]

A question posed toward the end of each session, aiming to elicit views on which part of the U.S. government should lead foreign policy efforts, garnered a variety of replies but not much discussion. More than one participant observed (correctly) that American foreign policy is led by the President, while a few commented that the National Security Council

---

[103] Focus group 13, West, March 25, 2021, transcript, p. 53.

[104] Focus group 14, Northeast, March 30, 2021, transcript, p. 47.

[105] Focus group 11, South, March 17, 2021, transcript, p. 55.

[106] Focus group 6, West, February 11, 2021, transcript, p. 48; focus group 11, South, March 17, 2021, transcript, p. 50.

[107] Focus group 1, Northeast, December 14, 2020, transcript, p. 24.

[108] Focus group 3, Northeast, February 2, 2021, transcript, p. 47.

[109] Focus group 5, South, February 9, 2021, transcript, p. 40.

[110] Focus group 11, South, March 17, 2021, transcript, p. 15.

[111] Focus group 6, West, February 11, 2021, transcript, p. 50.

[112] Focus group 9, Midwest, March 11, 2021, transcript, p. 48.

[113] Focus group 7, West, March 4, 2021, transcript, p. 53.

should coordinate the administration's efforts[114] or that the State Department should lead "under the President's direction."[115]

Similarly, participants seemed generally unsure as to whether the United States should spend more, less, or about the same amount on diplomacy, and there was no clear consensus. Several commented that it would be good to have more transparency and accountability on spending for foreign affairs at all levels.[116] Some participants argued for less spending and the need to prioritize spending at home instead.[117] Others could see spending more, if it was "wisely used"[118] or suggested that funding be transferred from military purposes.[119] Among the reasons given for the need to increase spending were "repairing international relationships,"[120] globalization necessitating increased cooperation,[121] and investment for protecting Americans abroad from climate change disasters.[122] Other participants supported keeping funding the same, generally expressing a belief that "they already spend a lot of money"[123] but that "you never know what could occur in the future that could have required you to at least have some sort of presence."[124]

## Awareness of the Foreign Service

Many participants (37 percent) indicated on the screening questionnaire that they were "not too familiar" with the Foreign Service. Although the majority (55 percent) of participants rated themselves as "somewhat familiar," there was a general lack of knowledge or understanding of the topic beyond the major points noted above. Each focus group discussion surfaced views similar to "Americans don't really pay too much attention until it affects their pocketbooks or it affects their lives directly on a day-to-day basis and their family."[125] Coping

---

[114] Focus group 7, West, March 4, 2021, transcript, p. 54.

[115] Focus group 11, South, March 17, 2021, transcript, p. 53.

[116] E.g., focus group 6, West, February 11, 2021, transcript, p. 54; focus group 8, South, March 9, 2021, transcript, p. 54.

[117] E.g., focus group 2, Northeast, December 17, 2020, transcript, p. 28; focus group 5, South, February 9, 2021, transcript, p. 46.

[118] Focus group 7, West, March 4, 2021, transcript, p. 57.

[119] Focus group 13, West, March 25, 2021, transcript, p. 52.

[120] E.g., focus group 5, South, February 9, 2021, transcript, p. 47.

[121] E.g., focus group 10, Midwest, March 15, 2021, transcript, p. 19.

[122] E.g., focus group 11, South, March 17, 2021, transcript, p. 55.

[123] Focus group 11, South, March 17, 2021, transcript, p. 54.

[124] Focus group 2, Northeast, December 17, 2020, transcript, p. 29.

[125] Focus group 3, Northeast, February 2, 2021, transcript, p. 15.

with daily work and family stressors meant for many[126] that the Foreign Service was simply "out of sight, out of mind,"[127] that it was unclear how diplomacy affected them,[128] and that people would only begin to pay attention when things went wrong,[129] such as after the September 11 terrorist attack.[130]

In general, many participants expressed in the discussions that they did not know what "diplomats do"[131] and that "not as much information [is] being shared."[132] One participant suggested that "if information is displayed somewhere or provided somewhere, say like in a government website, I think that would be helpful."[133] Some participants pointed to a general reluctance to follow world affairs because it seems like they did not impact their "day-to-day lives."[134]

One participant noted, "Americans know what firemen do, what policemen do. Engineers. Doctors. Lawyers. Not many people know what diplomats do."[135] Another said, "You understand that the embassies are there, but you don't understand . . . the intended or direct impact they have."[136] Another asked:

> How would the average person know about American diplomats? . . . Only if they're watching the news and only if there's something going on in the world that that diplomat is standing in front of the camera giving the American perspective. That's the only time you see them.[137]

Many people indicated that their understanding of diplomats and the Foreign Service came from representations in movies, television shows, or novels.[138] The images presented

---

[126] E.g., focus group 3, Northeast, February 2, 2021, transcript, p. 16; focus group 7, West, March 4, 2021, transcript, p. 3; focus group 11, South, March 17, 2021, transcript, p. 21.

[127] Focus group 4, Midwest, February 4, 2021, transcript, p. 19.

[128] E.g., focus group 8, South, March 9, 2021, transcript, p. 25; focus group 10, Midwest, March 15, 2021, transcript, p. 15.

[129] E.g., focus group 1, Northeast, December 14, 2020, transcript, p. 10; focus group 8, South, March 9, 2021, transcript, p. 11.

[130] E.g., focus group 3, Northeast, February 2, 2021, transcript, p. 14.

[131] Focus group 8, South, March 9, 2021, transcript, p. 21.

[132] Focus group 8, South, March 9, 2021, transcript, p. 21.

[133] Focus group 8, South, March 9, 2021, transcript, p. 23.

[134] E.g., focus group 8, South, March 9, 2021, transcript, p. 23.

[135] Focus group 2, Northeast, December 17, 2020, transcript, p. 18.

[136] Focus group 3, Northeast, February 2, 2021, transcript, p. 20.

[137] Focus group 11, South, March 17, 2021, transcript, p. 31.

[138] E.g., focus group 2, Northeast, December 17, 2020, transcript, p. 15; focus group 3, Northeast, February 2, 2021, transcript, p. 21; focus group 4, Midwest, February 4, 2021, transcript, p. 14; focus group 5, South, February 9, 2021, transcript, p. 28.

in the examples given included spies and espionage, abuse of diplomatic immunity, or that "everybody's in that building just sitting around waiting for someone in trouble to come running to them before they act."[139]

Travel was a common touchpoint for how focus group members conceptualized the ideas of diplomacy and the Foreign Service. The ability to seek help at embassies when traveling abroad was widely perceived to be a key benefit of diplomacy and the Foreign Service. One participant specifically thought that "customer service" was an important skill for diplomats in light of this role.[140] Other respondents judged the success of American diplomacy by how strongly they felt the need to locate the embassy during their travel planning.[141] One participant noted that the only aspect of the Foreign Service where they could assess how well things were going was in terms of helping tourists, because that was the only visible piece.[142]

While awareness and knowledge were generally low, there was a recurring theme that people are entitled to more information about the Foreign Service if they choose to seek it out, but that they did not know where to look. One participant noted:

> Considering we all pay federal taxes and it's supposed to represent us and everything like that, I think we should hear more...There's not as much information being shared. . . . It probably would mitigate the issue if there was potentially an outlet to seek this information.[143]

Similarly, in the discussion of whether or not American diplomacy is effective, a participant remarked,

> I don't know how you would typically hear about this or find out about this unless you were extremely politically active and very abreast of what's happening in the country and following all that. I don't know where you would go to find this information.[144]

## Views on Political Appointees Versus Career Diplomats

As noted in the previous chapter, focus group participants often made unsolicited comparisons between career diplomats and political appointees. While many participants generally rated their opinion of diplomats as being positive, several felt less positively about appointees

---

[139] Focus group 11, South, March 17, 2021, transcript, p. 23.

[140] Focus group 1, Northeast, December 14, 2020, transcript, p. 22.

[141] E.g., focus group 1, Northeast, December 14, 2020, transcript, p. 8.

[142] Focus group 8, South, March 9, 2021, transcript, p. 14.

[143] Focus group 8, South, March 9, 2021, transcript, p. 21.

[144] Focus group 4, Midwest, February 4, 2021, transcript, p. 16.

and assumed that they were less qualified, less dedicated, and less likely to be working in the taxpayers' interest.[145] Some participants expressed stronger concerns about appointees, stating that it was possible that they "don't really understand the process of the need to be culturally aware of the place . . . [They] wouldn't know what is respect versus disrespect. . . . If you put the wrong person in the position, it could mean war for us."[146] Despite these concerns, only rarely was it suggested by participants that political donors or appointees should be excluded from eligibility for service.[147]

Note that, with the addition of a question on the 2021 ALP survey, respondents were asked explicitly about their views of effectiveness of career and appointed diplomats in order to derive generalizable results. Results of that question appear in Figure 2.11.

## Summary of Focus Group Results

In moderated conversations intended to explore the ways that individuals think and speak about American diplomats and the Foreign Service, participants provided a variety of views on American diplomacy and the work of U.S. diplomats. Few of the focus group participants reported closely following international news, and in the discussions there seldom were references to ongoing or recent international issues. Overall, however, focus group participants had favorable, though perhaps hazy, views of American diplomacy.

When asked what came first to mind as the role of diplomacy, the focus group discussions typically began by pointing to protection of American citizens traveling abroad, followed by a general idea of building and maintaining relations with other countries. When asked whether American diplomacy is successful, participants generally pointed to a lack to news about it as an indicator of success. Some noted that domestic political polarization and discord had consequences in securing international cooperation abroad.

Focus group participants broadly considered peace, along with building relations and staying informed, as top goals for diplomacy. As for diplomatic tasks considered to be important, groups most commonly highlighted protecting American citizens abroad. Some participants had had first-hand experiences in getting help from embassy officers; others had heard second-hand of such experiences from friends or relatives. When presented with a list of tasks of diplomats, participants seemed not to know very much of the export promotion function, and some considered the role of promoting American values to be freighted by domestic American politics.

For the selection of American diplomats, participants highlighted the importance of language fluency but also placed value on bravery, negotiating skills, communication, and lead-

---

[145] E.g., focus group 3, Northeast, February 2, 2021, transcript, p. 29; focus group 8, South, March 9, 2021, transcript, p. 39; focus group 10, Midwest, March 15, 2021, transcript, p. 12.

[146] Focus group 5, South, February 9, 2021, transcript, p. 30.

[147] E.g., focus group 8, South, March 9, 2021, transcript, p. 47.

ership skills as top factors to consider. While some participants saw value in having diplomats spend time in the United States outside of Washington, participants overall held a wide range of views on the idea. Unprompted, participants brought up the role of political appointee (non-career) ambassadors, who were not thought to be as effective as career diplomats in the ambassadorial role.

CHAPTER FOUR

# Key Findings and Implications

As noted in Chapter One, prior surveys have examined subjects such as public attitudes toward American engagement in the world and perceptions of what the important goals of foreign policy should be. However, they generally have not examined attitudes toward the Foreign Service or its officers; what the public believes are the most important functions diplomats undertake; beliefs about how diplomats should be selected; or how much the nation should rely on political, non-career ambassadors relative to appointees.

Existing evidence indicates that the majority of Americans support the United States playing a shared leadership role in the world and that this is not a highly partisan belief. Prior surveys also identify that, since at least the early 2000s, the public believes that among the most important foreign policy goals are "protecting the jobs of American workers," "preventing the spread of nuclear weapons," and "combating international terrorism." In contrast with support for American leadership in the world, support for specific foreign policies do show partisan divides, with Democrats more likely to prioritize outward-facing policy goals and Republicans to prioritize inward goals. As a backdrop to these findings, a General Social Survey question from 2006 asked individuals whether they feel like they are informed about foreign policy: 52 percent indicated that they were "very" or "somewhat" informed, but 31 percent indicated that they were "somewhat" or "very" uninformed.[1]

This report is intended to address the gap in data on attitudes and beliefs about the State Department and American diplomats more specifically. Our findings are presented in this chapter as *key findings* from the data, from which we draw *implications* for the State Department, the administration, Congress, and others interested the topic.

## Key Findings

Overall public impressions of diplomacy and American diplomats by ALP respondents were *generally favorable*, though it emerged in the focus groups that most Americans know relatively little specifically about the Foreign Service, its functions, or how diplomats are chosen. The favorable attitude was stable between two nationwide data gathering efforts a year apart, with 37 percent of respondents having a favorable or very favorable view of American dip-

---

[1] T. Smith et al., 2019.

lomats in 2021, against only 5 percent with an unfavorable or very unfavorable opinion. But the "no opinion" response was significant as well, at 25 percent. Greater knowledge of the Foreign Service was associated with more favorable impressions, above and beyond sociodemographic differences in impressions.

## Diplomatic Functions and Skills

### Survey Results

When presented randomly ordered lists of the *major functions* of diplomats, ALP respondents were most aware of the function "helping citizens abroad." The two next most-cited functions for American diplomacy were to "report on developments" abroad and "advance American interests." On the other hand, in the nationwide ALP sample, respondents overall seemed least aware that American diplomats had any engagement with export promotion or business protection.

In the 2020 ALP survey, "promoting values" was in the middle range of function awareness, and less than 20 percent of respondents considered it important. To probe this question further, we added a specific question on values promotion to the 2021 ALP survey questionnaire. The question began with context that the "American values" in the question would include democracy, freedom, human rights, and the rule of law. Then respondents were asked, "How strongly do you agree or disagree with the statement: 'It is in America's interests to promote our values in today's world'?" More than 56 percent agreed or strongly agreed, and only 14 percent disagreed or disagreed strongly. We conclude from this that there is majority support for promotion of American values by our diplomats abroad and plurality support for budget increases when provided with information on current spending levels relative to the military.

We also asked ALP respondents to identify skills that they considered most important for diplomats to have by choosing from a list. "Understanding of global affairs" and "negotiating skill" were consistently rated as the two most important skills, while "public speaking," "bravery," "discipline in following instructions," and "empathy" were clustered at the low end.

### Focus Group Results

Across the focus groups, participants often admitted that they knew relatively little about the activities and contributions of American diplomats abroad. Some considered that to be a plus, as evidenced by the following statement: "[i]f you don't hear about it, it must be going well." Nonetheless, lively discussions were held on a range of topics in each group.

As in the survey responses, when presented with a list of the *major functions* of diplomats, focus group participants were most aware of the function "helping citizens abroad." Some participants could cite examples of having asked for help at embassies abroad (or they knew of friends and relatives who had needed and received help). This function was highly valued across the groups, with one participant explaining that it was important so that "we feel like when we're somewhere else, we have someplace to go" when problems come up.

In reaction to the two next most-cited important functions for American diplomacy from the ALP survey ("report on developments" abroad and "advance American interests"), focus group participants explained their importance as determining "what's really going on" abroad in an era of information overload and "developing relationships." In every in-depth discussion of this point in the focus groups, participants endorsed the idea that in-person diplomacy would continue to be important, perhaps even more important in the future. Participants emphasized the need for relationships and linked that to achieving peace.

As with the ALP survey, focus groups overall seemed least aware that American diplomats had any engagement with export promotion or business protection.

In the focus groups, we were able to tease out some reasons that might explain the relatively low-ranked importance of "promoting U.S. values and culture" in the surveys; some participants said that they considered "values" to be a "loaded term," divisive in domestic political contexts, or that this activity could be imposing ways of thinking that were not always welcome in other countries.

The discussions of diplomats' skills in the focus groups were more nuanced than the data captured in the survey, particularly as a result of conversational give and take within the groups related to the concept of diversity. Language fluency was often cited as important and related to success in negotiating.

## Association of Favorability and Respondents' Demographic Factors
### Survey Results

The ALP survey allowed us to probe differences in favorable and unfavorable ratings (and responses to other questions) by demographic and political view characteristics. For the general favorability question, we found that men were significantly more likely to have a favorable or very favorable opinion of the Foreign Service than women (women had significantly higher "no opinion" answers, not higher "unfavorable" scores). Respondents with higher incomes or higher educational attainments, as well as those who reported voting in 2016, were more likely to view American diplomats favorably. Interestingly, political views along a continuum from very liberal to very conservative were not linked to overall perceptions of favorability.

Demographic factors also can be linked to which diplomatic functions were considered more or less important. Older respondents were more likely to consider "advancing interests" and "promoting values" to be important, while younger respondents considered "negotiating" more important. Among those with higher incomes and educational attainment, "advancing interests," "promoting values," and "negotiating" were relatively more important. Those with lower educational attainment and lower incomes prioritized "helping sell products," "determining visas," and "fighting crime and terrorism." One interpretation of these data is that older and higher-income individuals were more supportive of *proactive* functions, while lower-socioeconomic-status groups emphasized *defensive or protective* functions.

## Perceptions of Diplomats

### Survey Results

ALP respondents were asked in both 2020 and 2021 whether they considered American diplomats to be "broadly representative" of American society. Consistent with limited direct knowledge of the Foreign Service, most respondents (55–60 percent) in both years had "no opinion" on the question. But of those with opinions, in 2020 a slight majority considered diplomats to be representative of American society, while in 2021, there was a statistically significant 8-percent increase (and a majority) of those with opinions who thought that diplomats were *not* representative.

Respondents were also asked whether they considered American diplomats to be "trustworthy" or (separately) "politically biased." As with the representativeness question, about half of participants had no opinion. But, paradoxically, among those with opinions, most respondents considered diplomats to be both "trustworthy" *and* "politically biased." The results were similar in 2020 and 2021.

In order to evaluate concerns about appointed ambassadors compared with career ambassadors that emerged during focus groups discussions, we added a question to the 2021 ALP survey. It gave background on the political appointment process and noted that both types of ambassadors are charged with representing administration policies. Then the question was asked whether career or political appointees would likely be more or equally effective at a series of tasks (e.g., "represent interests," "report on developments," "explain the U.S."). Career ambassadors were consistently considered to be more effective at such tasks than political ambassadors.

### Focus Group Results

While the focus group discussions contained many examples of assumed trustworthiness, reflecting the survey results, they did not surface an in-depth discussion of the political bias notion.

The focus groups saw lively discussions of the importance of diversity. A few participants suggested that demographic characteristics should not factor into selection criteria for diplomats and that they should be chosen on the basis of exam scores alone. But more participants saw the value of a diverse Foreign Service that would give diplomats more cultural sensitivity and awareness and also would "look more like America." (This may have been related to views of political bias, addressed below.)

In many of the focus groups, distinctions between career and politically appointed ambassadors were brought up, unprompted by the moderator. In these sessions, most participants said that they felt less positively about political appointees than career ambassadors. They felt that appointees were less qualified, less dedicated, and less likely to be working in the public interest, among other opinions. This was subsequently echoed in the representative survey data.

## Diplomacy and National Security

### Survey Results

We examined the relationship of diplomacy to national security in the ALP survey. A strong and consistent majority (over 65 percent) thought that diplomacy contributes to national security. A related issue was perceptions of the relationships between the military and diplomacy in the U.S. national security toolbox. In the survey, we asked directly whether respondents thought diplomats or the military "should lead efforts abroad." A consistent plurality (43 percent in 2020 and 44 percent in 2021) in both administrations of the survey said that diplomats should lead, though a little over one-third of respondents had no opinion. Only one-fifth of respondents said that the military should lead.

### Focus Group Results

The focus groups illuminated some of the reasons that may be behind the survey responses. First, related to national security, participants thought that diplomacy would allow the nation to negotiate and avoid armed conflicts and solve global problems together with other countries (climate change and pandemics were commonly mentioned examples). Several focus group participants emphasized the complexity and volatility of today's world, which they argued required more engagement and diplomacy to manage.

When we probed on the question of whether diplomats or the military should lead most efforts abroad in the focus groups, across groups it was most commonly concluded that it was better for diplomats to lead in most cases because diplomats "promote peace" and other countries see the military as "aggressive." Focus group participants did qualify their replies, noting that the United States should not rely on diplomats to deal with ISIS "because they wouldn't do" what we might ask. That is a job for the military, it was said. In the focus groups, moderators also sought to elicit views on which parts of the U.S. government should lead in the formulation of American foreign policy, but participants did not engage much, beyond generally affirming that the President should lead in the foreign policy process.

## Spending on Diplomacy

### Survey Results

Finally, our initial findings related to perceptions of funding for the State Department were consistent with earlier results from Pew Research Center. Among respondents, there was a general preference for keeping spending about the same, with somewhat more support among the rest for cutting than for adding to funding.

During the focus group discussions, it emerged that participants had generally no point of reference for what kind of funding the State Department currently received. Therefore, for the second ALP survey, we modified the spending question for half of the sample to inform respondents that, since 2010, about 1.2 percent to 1.5 percent of the federal budget has gone to the State Department. In contrast with respondents who did not receive the additional information, there was a statistically significant increase of 9 percentage points among those who favored increasing foreign affairs funding, a 36-percent increase in support for increased funding. Even with the altered presentation of the question, however, nearly half of the respondents favored keeping funding the same.

### Focus Group Results

As noted above, we found that focus group participants had relatively little confidence in participating in discussions aimed at understanding whether public opinion favored more, less, or about the same spending on foreign affairs. Participants expressed a plurality of ideas with no clear consensus, potentially because participants generally lacked information on the scope of funding that the State Department currently receives.

## Implications

Our study has documented generally favorable public opinion attitudes toward American diplomats but also found limited understanding of what diplomats actually do, how they are selected, and how diplomacy interacts with other elements of America's national security establishment. One clear implication is that more public understanding is needed.

The State Department already appears to realize the need for more outreach to and communication with the American people, consistent with legal restrictions mainly aimed at materials such as Voice of America broadcasts.[2] Secretary Michael Pompeo spoke widely around the country during his tenure (2018–2021), though he did receive criticism for it.[3] In an address on October 27, 2021, on the modernization of American diplomacy, Secretary of State Antony Blinken explained the importance of public support to the work of the State Department:

> We also want to hear more from the American people. Our mission is to deliver for them and all those who have an equity in the work that we do. Too often our communication is a one-way street. We talk and we hope they listen. We've got to do more listening. And that's not just the right thing to do. It's the necessary thing to do. Because if key

---

[2] The United States Information and Educational Exchange Act of 1948 (U.S. Code, Title 22, United States Information and Educational Exchange Act of 1948 [Smith-Mundt Act], Section 1431, Congressional Declaration of Objectives, 1948) restricted any information materials produced by the U.S. Information Agency, and later the State Department, to overseas distribution only. In 2012, the Smith-Mundt Modernization Act was incorporated into the National Defense Authorization Act for 2013 (H.R. 4310, Section 1078). Recognizing the ubiquity of the internet and social media, the amendments allowed for materials "intended for foreign audiences" also to be available to domestic audiences. But the act also states (Section 206) that "no funds" authorized to the State Department and the Broadcasting Board of Governors "shall be used to influence public opinion in the United States." See also John Hudson, "U.S. Repeals Propaganda Ban, Spreads Government-Made News to Americans," *Foreign Policy*, July 14, 2013.

[3] See, e.g., Carol Morello, "Pompeo Accused of Mixing Politics and Diplomacy as Election Nears," *Washington Post*, October 5, 2020.

stakeholders aren't with us on the takeoff, they're less likely to stick with us on the landing. We need their ideas, and we need their buy-in.

So, I'll be asking all senior officials to make domestic travel and engagement a greater priority, and that includes senior leaders at posts who can engage virtually. We're going to reach out much more regularly to civil society groups, private companies, state and local governments, community organizations, universities, and we'll make sure that we're communicating with people from different parts of the country—urban and rural—because our mission isn't to serve some Americans, but all Americans. We're diplomats, and we're going to focus more of our diplomacy here at home to make sure our policies reflect the needs, the aspirations, the values of the American people.[4]

Our research findings suggest that such measures as Secretary Blinken proposes will increase understanding and support around the country for diplomacy and for those who carry it out.

There are other implications of this study. Our study respondents clearly considered support for American citizens abroad as a core—and much-valued—function for diplomats. This suggests that further strengthening this bond by improving services to American citizens traveling abroad would pay considerable dividends to the State Department and the traveling public as well. While there were significant problems with the withdrawal from Afghanistan in August–September 2021, prompting multiple Inspector General investigations,[5] State Department officials and the United States military performed heroically during the evacuation of citizens and U.S.-associated Afghans from Kabul. In his speech cited above, Secretary Blinken also announced a serious lessons-learned examination of that crisis. While possibly controversial, such an examination could help convince public opinion of the seriousness with which the State Department takes support for citizens abroad.

We documented that the general public was somewhat surprised to learn that diplomats abroad have responsibilities toward export promotion and business support. One clear implication of this is for embassies and the Department of State to be much more public about the support and advocacy provided to businesses, including farmers. Ambassadors should seek opportunities to articulate the advantages of American companies and visit American-owned or American-associated facilities abroad and at home. State Department economic officers should be ready to take part in domestic business and labor conferences, perhaps more feasible now with widespread virtual conferencing tools, to help them explain opportunities while abroad. Social media can also help get the word out.

Among functions carried out by diplomats, the importance placed on promoting American "values" abroad by survey respondents and focus group participants was lower than

---

[4] U.S. Department of State, "Secretary Antony J. Blinken on the Modernization of American Diplomacy," press release, October 27, 2021b.

[5] See, e.g., Lara Seligman, Andrew Desiderio, and Nahal Toosi, "State IG Launches Investigations into End of Afghanistan Operations," *Politico*, October 18, 2021.

might be expected. Survey respondents rated it near the bottom of important functions, and participants in some focus groups debated the meaning of "American values" and the appropriateness of such activities. But in the second ALP survey, which specified what was meant by "values," respondents were more supportive of this function. This finding suggests that American officials should be more explicit at home about the values being promoted abroad and why.

We found increasing concern about whether the Foreign Service was "representative" of American society. This may reflect the broader awareness of "diversity" or the increase in positive views about diversity.[6] This also echoes Secretary Condoleezza Rice's earlier call for and promotion of "transformational diplomacy" that aimed to strengthen the State Department and American diplomacy during her term (2005–2009):

> Ladies and gentlemen, in order for America to fully play its role in the world, it must send out into the world a diplomatic corps that reflects that great diversity. It cannot be that the last three Secretaries of State—the daughter of European immigrants, the son of Jamaican immigrants and a daughter of the American segregated South—would be more diverse than the Foreign Service with which they work. . . . But we cannot do it without America's best and brightest, and America's best and brightest come in all colors, they come in all religions, they come in all heritages. Our Foreign Service has got to be that way, too.[7]

An implication of our findings is that the State Department should make a more public and vigorous effort to improve representation among the ranks for its diplomats and that such efforts would also be aligned with public concern.

Similarly, the study showed worrisome levels of opinion that American diplomats, while considered "trustworthy," were also thought to be "politically biased." This suggests that the Department should undertake a dedicated effort to reinforce nonpartisanship among its officials. The study's finding that the American public has greater confidence in career ambassadors than political appointees also implies that the public would support reduced numbers of appointees in State Department positions.

As described earlier, our experiment in providing just one sentence on the relative funding for the State Department in the second administration of the survey yielded a statistically significant increase in support for additional funding, compared with a control group of respondents who did not receive that information. Consistent with other findings here illustrating the need for greater knowledge among the public, this suggests that greater efforts to inform the public on relative funding for the foreign affairs budget, and transparency about how the spending is used, would lead to greater public support for such budgetary allocations.

---

[6] Abby Budiman, "Americans Are More Positive About the Long-Term Rise in U.S. Racial and Ethnic Diversity Than in 2016," Washington, D.C.: Pew Research Center, October 1, 2020.

[7] U.S. Department of State, "Transformational Diplomacy," speech by Condoleezza Rice, Georgetown University, Washington, D.C., January 18, 2006.

Finally, the survey data illuminated a two-to-one preference for diplomats (among those with a preference), as opposed to military leaders, to lead foreign relations—although 36 percent of respondents indicated that they did not know who should lead. This suggests support for a higher public profile to ambassadors and Department officials abroad in situations of crisis and non-crisis alike. And it suggests that Secretary Blinken's initiative to get senior officials out domestically talking to, and listening to, the American public will build support for American diplomacy.

## Conclusion

This report has focused on American opinions regarding the U.S. Foreign Service, diplomats, and diplomacy, and it has provided a glimpse into public opinion. As noted in Chapter One, previous research focused on American attitudes toward international engagement, the desired U.S. role in foreign affairs, and perceptions of important foreign policy goals. We hope that researchers and policymakers will consider our findings in light of previous studies and follow up on these findings to evaluate their validity and ongoing dynamics as the United States engages in vital relationships with the wider world.

APPENDIX A

# American Life Panel Survey (Wave 1, 2020)

*We would like to ask you a series of questions about U.S. embassies abroad and Americans who serve as diplomats in them.*

Q1. Do you have a U.S. passport?
- Yes
- No

[If yes,] Q2. Have you travelled outside the United States in the last 10 years?
- Yes
- No

[If yes,] Q3. How often have you travelled outside of the country in the last 10 years?
Fewer than 5 trips ___
5–10 trips ___
More than 10 ___

Q4. Have you ever visited a U.S. embassy for help or information?
- Yes
- No

Q5. Have you ever visited a U.S. embassy website or State.gov for help or information?
- Yes (1)
- No (2)

Q6. Would you say your overall impression of American diplomats and U.S. embassies abroad is:
- Very favorable (1)
- Favorable (2)
- Neutral (3)
- Negative (4)
- Very negative (5)
- No opinion (6)

*Q7. American diplomats staff 307 embassies, consulates, and missions all over the world, mostly accompanied by their families, at times in remote and dangerous cities abroad. In war zones, they serve alongside the U.S. military. They are selected through a competitive exam process that tests global knowledge and judgment.*

American diplomats abroad do all of the following things. Please indicate *if you already knew* that they . . .

| | Yes (1) | No (2) |
|---|---|---|
| help U.S. citizens traveling or living abroad who are in trouble (e.g., in case of arrest, disaster, or other emergencies) (1) | ○ | ○ |
| advance American interests with foreign governments and foreign citizens, including on national security matters (2) | ○ | ○ |
| report on developments in the countries where they are located that may affect the U.S. (3) | ○ | ○ |
| negotiate treaties and agreements (4) | ○ | ○ |
| help U.S. companies and farmers sell American products (5) | ○ | ○ |
| decide on applications for visas for travel to the U.S. (6) | ○ | ○ |
| promote and explain U.S. values and culture to encourage positive views of the U.S. and the American people. (7) | ○ | ○ |

Q8. Which do you think are the most important functions of diplomats? [list randomized] *Please choose 3 only.*
- ❏ Advance American interests with foreign governments (1)
- ❏ Help U.S. citizens in trouble (2)
- ❏ Help businesses sell U.S. products (3)
- ❏ Decide who can travel to the U.S. (4)
- ❏ Promote U.S. values and culture (5)
- ❏ Negotiate treaties and agreements (6)
- ❏ Work to fight international crime, drug trafficking, and terrorism (7)
- ❏ Promote scientific cooperation against global threats such as pandemics (8)
- ❏ Represent the U.S. in United Nations (U.N.) and other international organizations (9)
- ❏ Other [Specify] (10) _____

Q9. What do you think are the two most important skills for diplomats to have? [list randomized]
Please rank top two.
\_\_\_ Success in advancing U.S. interests (1)
\_\_\_Understanding of global affairs (2)
\_\_\_Language fluency (3)
\_\_\_Negotiating skill (4)
\_\_\_Bravery in face of danger (5)
\_\_\_ Discipline in following instructions (6)
\_\_\_ Skill in public speaking/press affairs (7)
\_\_\_ Familiarity with U.S. politics (8)
\_\_\_ Empathy (9)
\_\_\_ Other [Specify] (10) _____

Q10. Do you consider American diplomats to be trustworthy?
- Yes (1)
- No (2)
- Don't know/No opinion (3)

Q11. In your view, are American diplomats politically biased?
- Yes (1)
- No (2)
- Don't know/No opinion (3)

Q12. From what you know, do you think our diplomats are representative of the United States in terms of racial and gender diversity and regional and socioeconomic backgrounds?
- Diplomats are broadly representative (1)
- Diplomats are not representative (2)
- Don't know/No opinion (3)

Q13. Do you think that our diplomacy contributes to our national security?
- Yes (1)
- No (2)
- Don't know/No opinion (3)

Q14. Do you think that diplomats or the military should lead U.S. efforts in most countries abroad?
- Diplomats (1)
- Military (2)
- Don't know/No opinion (3)

Q15. Do you think that face-to-face diplomacy in order to represent the country and protect Americans in harm's way is effective or necessary in the digital age?
- ○ Face-to-face diplomacy is important these days. (1)
- ○ Face-to-face diplomacy is not very important these days. (2)
- ○ Don't know/No opinion (3)

Q16. Please tell me how much confidence you have in the ability of leaders in each of these institutions to shape policies that benefit the United States:

|  | A great deal | A fair amount | Not very much | No confidence at all |
|---|---|---|---|---|
| The military | ○ | ○ | ○ | ○ |
| U.S. State Department | ○ | ○ | ○ | ○ |
| Intelligence agencies | ○ | ○ | ○ | ○ |
| Congress | ○ | ○ | ○ | ○ |
| Think tanks | ○ | ○ | ○ | ○ |
| Academia | ○ | ○ | ○ | ○ |
| The White House | ○ | ○ | ○ | ○ |
| Large corporations | ○ | ○ | ○ | ○ |
| The media | ○ | ○ | ○ | ○ |

Q17. How important a role do you think the following currently play in determining the foreign policy of the United States—a very important role, a somewhat important role, or hardly an important role at all?

|  | Very important | Somewhat important | Hardly important | Not sure |
|---|---|---|---|---|
| The President | ○ | ○ | ○ | ○ |
| Secretary of State | ○ | ○ | ○ | ○ |
| State Department as a whole | ○ | ○ | ○ | ○ |
| Congress | ○ | ○ | ○ | ○ |
| The military | ○ | ○ | ○ | ○ |
| Public opinion | ○ | ○ | ○ | ○ |
| American business | ○ | ○ | ○ | ○ |
| The CIA | ○ | ○ | ○ | ○ |
| National Security Advisor | ○ | ○ | ○ | ○ |

Q18. If you were making up the budget for the federal government next year (2021), would you increase spending, decrease spending, or keep spending the same for the State Department and American embassies?
- ○ Increase spending
- ○ Decrease spending
- ○ Keep spending the same

APPENDIX B

# American Life Panel Survey (Wave 2, 2021)

We would like to ask you a series of questions about U.S. embassies abroad and Americans who serve as diplomats in them.

Q4. Have you ever visited a U.S. embassy for help or information?
- ○ Yes (1)
- ○ No (2)

Q5. Have you ever visited a U.S. embassy website or State.gov for help or information?
- ○ Yes (1)
- ○ No (2)

Q6. Would you say your overall impression of American diplomats and U.S. embassies abroad is:
- ○ Very favorable (1)
- ○ Favorable (2)
- ○ Neutral (3)
- ○ Negative (4)
- ○ Very negative (5)
- ○ No opinion (6)

Q7. American diplomats staff 307 embassies, consulates, and missions all over the world, mostly accompanied by their families, at times in remote and dangerous cities abroad. In war zones, they serve alongside the U.S. military. They are selected through a competitive exam process that tests global knowledge and judgment.

American diplomats abroad do all of the following things.
*Please indicate if you already knew that they . . .*

|  | Yes (1) | No (2) |
|---|---|---|
| help U.S. citizens traveling or living abroad who are in trouble (e.g., in case of arrest, disaster, or other emergencies) (1) | ○ | ○ |
| advance American interests with foreign governments and foreign citizens, including on national security matters (2) | ○ | ○ |
| report on developments in the countries where they are located that may affect the U.S. (3) | ○ | ○ |
| negotiate treaties and agreements (4) | ○ | ○ |
| help U.S. companies and farmers sell American products (5) | ○ | ○ |
| decide on applications for visas for travel to the U.S. (6) | ○ | ○ |
| promote and explain U.S. values and culture to encourage positive views of the U.S. and the American people. (7) | ○ | ○ |

Q8. Which do you think are the most important functions of diplomats?
*Please choose 3 only.*

- ❏ Advance American interests with foreign governments (1)
- ❏ Help U.S. citizens in trouble (2)
- ❏ Help businesses sell U.S. products (3)
- ❏ Decide who can travel to the U.S. (4)
- ❏ Promote U.S. values and culture (5)
- ❏ Negotiate treaties and agreements (6)
- ❏ Work to fight international crime, drug trafficking, and terrorism (7)
- ❏ Promote scientific cooperation against global threats such as pandemics (8)
- ❏ Represent the U.S. in United Nations (U.N.) and other international organizations (9)
- ❏ Other [Specify] (10) _____

Q9. What do you think are the two most important skills for diplomats to have?
*Please rank top two.*

___ Success in advancing U.S. interests (1)
___ Understanding of global affairs (2)
___ Language fluency (3)
___ Negotiating skill (4)
___ Bravery in face of danger (5)
___ Discipline in following instructions (6)
___ Skill in public speaking/press affairs (7)
___ Familiarity with U.S. politics (8)
___ Empathy (9)
___ Other [Specify] (10) _____

Q10. Do you consider American diplomats to be trustworthy?
- Yes (1)
- No (2)
- Don't know/No opinion (3)

Q11. In your view, are American diplomats politically biased?
- Yes (1)
- No (2)
- Don't know/No opinion (3)

Q20. The United States has two types of ambassadors: (1) professional career diplomats, who are selected through a series of written and oral exams, and have different assignments for 20 years or more before their nomination, and (2) political appointees nominated by the President, who come from varying backgrounds and generally serve only during the President's term and resign when a new President is inaugurated. As ambassadors, both career diplomats and political appointees are personal representatives of the President abroad and are charged with representing administration policies.

Please select the answer that is closest to your opinion on who is more likely to be effective as ambassador at each of these goals:

|  | Career (1) | Appointed (2) | Equally effective (3) |
|---|---|---|---|
| Represent and protect the interests and citizens of the U.S. abroad (1) | ○ | ○ | ○ |
| Report on developments abroad, negotiate treaties and agreements (2) | ○ | ○ | ○ |
| Explain the U.S. to foreign audiences (3) | ○ | ○ | ○ |
| Promote U.S. exports and seek foreign investment for the U.S. (4) | ○ | ○ | ○ |
| Pursue friendly international relations (5) | ○ | ○ | ○ |

Q21. Some people say the United States has a unique character that makes it the greatest country in the world. Others say that every country is unique, and the United States is no greater than other nations. Which view is closer to your own?
- ○ The United States has a unique character that makes it the greatest country in the world. (1)
- ○ Every country is unique, and the United States is no greater than other nations. (2)

Q12. From what you know, do you think our diplomats are representative of the United States in terms of racial and gender diversity and regional and socioeconomic backgrounds?
- ○ Diplomats are broadly representative (1)
- ○ Diplomats are not representative (2)
- ○ Don't know/No opinion (3)

Q13. Do you think that our diplomacy contributes to our national security?
- ○ Yes (1)
- ○ No (2)
- ○ Don't know/No opinion (3)

Q14. Do you think that diplomats or the military should lead U.S. efforts in most countries abroad?
- ○ Diplomats (1)
- ○ Military (2)
- ○ Don't know/No opinion (3)

Q15. Do you think that face-to-face diplomacy in order to represent the country and protect Americans in harm's way is effective or necessary in the digital age?
- ○ Face-to-face diplomacy is important these days. (1)
- ○ Face-to-face diplomacy is not very important these days. (2)
- ○ Don't know/No opinion (3)

Q16. Please tell me how much confidence you have in the ability of leaders in each of these institutions to shape policies that benefit the United States:

|  | A great deal (1) | A fair amount (2) | Not very much (3) | No confidence at all (4) |
|---|---|---|---|---|
| The military (1) | ○ | ○ | ○ | ○ |
| U.S. State Department (2) | ○ | ○ | ○ | ○ |
| Intelligence agencies (3) | ○ | ○ | ○ | ○ |
| Congress (4) | ○ | ○ | ○ | ○ |
| Think tanks (5) | ○ | ○ | ○ | ○ |
| Academia (6) | ○ | ○ | ○ | ○ |
| The White House (7) | ○ | ○ | ○ | ○ |
| Large corporations (8) | ○ | ○ | ○ | ○ |
| The media (9) | ○ | ○ | ○ | ○ |

Q17. How important a role do you think the following currently play in determining the foreign policy of the United States—a very important role, a somewhat important role, or hardly an important role at all?

|  | Very important (1) | Somewhat important (2) | Hardly important (3) | Not sure (4) |
|---|---|---|---|---|
| The President (1) | ○ | ○ | ○ | ○ |
| Secretary of State (2) | ○ | ○ | ○ | ○ |
| State Department as a whole (3) | ○ | ○ | ○ | ○ |
| Congress (4) | ○ | ○ | ○ | ○ |
| The military (5) | ○ | ○ | ○ | ○ |
| Public opinion (6) | ○ | ○ | ○ | ○ |
| American business (7) | ○ | ○ | ○ | ○ |
| The CIA (8) | ○ | ○ | ○ | ○ |
| National Security Advisor (9) | ○ | ○ | ○ | ○ |

Q18. *[Half of respondents saw this first statement in addition to the second statement]* Since 2010, about 1.2 percent–1.5 percent of the federal budget has gone to the State Department and American embassies. For comparison, about 15–20 percent of the federal budget has gone to the U.S. military during this time.

If you were making up the budget for the federal government next year (2022), would you increase spending, decrease spending, or keep spending the same for the State Department and American embassies?

- ○ Increase spending (1)
- ○ Decrease spending (2)
- ○ Keep spending the same (3)

Q19. In many periods of American history, our diplomats have promoted American values, as well as interests, abroad. Americans have believed that the U.S. would be more secure and more prosperous in a world in which our values such as democracy, freedom, human rights, and the rule of law were more widespread among other countries.

How strongly do you agree or disagree with the statement:

"It is in America's interests to promote our values in today's world."

- ○ Strongly agree (1)
- ○ Agree (2)
- ○ Neutral (3)
- ○ Disagree (4)
- ○ Strongly disagree (5)

APPENDIX C

# Selected Detailed Results

## Methodological Approach

In this appendix, we outline our approach to analyze the RAND ALP data to examine the relationship between a range of sociodemographic and other background factors and perceptions of the Foreign Service and U.S. diplomats and present several tables of complete regression results to support interpretation of statements in the report. We consider perceptions that are either continuous variables (such as number of diplomatic functions that are known by respondents) or that are binary (such as whether the overall impression of the Foreign Service is positive or not). When examining links between demographic variables and continuous perceptions, we use an Ordinary Least Squares regression in which the regression coefficient for each variable can be interpreted as the change in the perception measure associated with a one-unit change in [the demographic variable]. When examining links between demographic variables and binary perceptions, we use logistic regression to identify the relationship between the odds of the perception (such as a positive impression of the Foreign Service compared with any other impression) and a set of sociodemographic variables.

## Computing Odds Ratios

To assist with interpreting the relationships between the background covariates and the binary perception items, the results in the logistic regression tables are shown in odds ratios. Odds ratios represent the odds of having a perception—a positive impression, for example—relative to not having that perception, and the odds ratio is shown for each covariate and its associated categories (e.g., male or female for gender). As an example, for the variable gender, the odds ratio is interpreted as the odds of the perception being held for a gender category (e.g., male) compared with the odds of it being held for an excluded category for that same variable (e.g., female). The excluded category is typically set to 1, and the other categories are interpreted relative to 1. If the odds ratio for that category (e.g., male) is greater than 1, then there are higher odds of the perception occurring for that category compared with the excluded category (in this case, female). If the odds ratio is less than 1, then there are lower odds of the outcome of interest occurring associated with that category.

## Sociodemographic and Other Background Variables

Of the initial 2,026 respondents to the first ALP survey, 1,829 also participated in the second survey. For the analyses in this report, we include only respondents who participated in both surveys. Table C.1 presents the unweighted proportions and means of the background variables used in the analyses for all respondents in each wave of the ALP survey to permit comparison of the sample over time. Unweighted wave 1 and 2 characteristics are similar, with no statistical differences in the sample at wave 1 and at wave 2. However, as noted in the report, once survey weights are applied, wave 2 participation was statistically significantly lower for younger, lower-income, and non-Hispanic black individuals.

**TABLE C.1**
**Proportions and Means of Unweighted Sociodemographic and Other Background Variables, by Wave**

| Variable | Wave 1 | Wave 2 |
|---|---|---|
| Gender | | |
| Male | 44.1 | 44.6 |
| Female | 55.9 | 55.4 |
| Race/ethnicity | | |
| Non-Hispanic white | 74.3 | 75.2 |
| Non-Hispanic black | 8.0 | 7.5 |
| Non-Hispanic other | 4.9 | 4.9 |
| Hispanic | 12.8 | 12.4 |
| Age (in years) | 59.3 | 59.5 |
| College degree or higher | 53.9 | 54.7 |
| Income (in $1,000s) | 82.1 | 83.2 |
| Urbanicity | | |
| Urban | 78.0 | 77.8 |
| Rural | 22.0 | 22.2 |
| Married | 61.0 | 61.6 |
| Voted in 2016 | 91.0 | 91.3 |
| Conservativism (range 1–5) | 3.0 | 3.0 |
| Knowledge of Foreign Service | 5.2 | 5.2 |
| | N = 2,026 | N = 1,829 |

# Selected Regression Results

ALP data are available free to registered users at alpdata.rand.org. Relevant surveys are ms545 (2020) and ms573 (2021). Complete regression results are available upon request.

**TABLE C.2**
**Results of Logistic Regressions for Increasing Perceived Importance of the Secretary of State in Determining Foreign Policy to "Very Important" in 2021 from Any Other Rating in 2020**

| Variable | |
|---|---|
| Gender | |
|     Female | 1 |
|     Male | 1.567 |
| | (1.33) |
| Race/ethnicity | |
|     Non-Hispanic white | 1 |
|     Non-Hispanic black | 2.537 |
| | (1.37) |
|     Non-Hispanic other | 2.222 |
| | (1.15) |
|     Hispanic | 1.087 |
| | (0.17) |
| Age (in years) | 1.022* |
| | (2.02) |
| Educational attainment | |
|     Less than a college degree | 1 |
|     College degree or higher | 1.937* |
| | (1.98) |
| Income (in $1,000s) | 1.007 |
| | (1.91) |
| Rural/urban residence | |
|     Urban | 1 |
|     Rural | 0.394* |
| | (−2.27) |

## Table C.2—Continued

| Variable | |
|---|---|
| Marital status | |
|     Not married | 1 |
|     Married | 0.953 |
| | (−0.13) |
| Election participation | |
|     Voted in 2016 | 1 |
|     Did not vote in 2016 | 1.165 |
| | (0.38) |
| Political conservatism | 0.971 |
| | (−0.18) |
| Observations | 768 |

NOTES: Results are shown in odds ratios with $t$ statistics in parentheses.

* $p < 0.05$, ** $p < 0.01$, *** $p < 0.001$.

## TABLE C.3
## Results of Logistic Regressions for Positive Overall Impression of American Diplomats and U.S. Embassies Abroad in 2020

| Variable | Regression Model 1: Positive Impression | Regression Model 2: Positive Impression[a] |
|---|---|---|
| Gender | | |
|   Female | 1 | 1 |
|   Male | 1.625* | 1.420 |
| | (2.39) | (1.71) |
| Race/ethnicity | | |
|   Non-Hispanic white | 1 | 1 |
|   Non-Hispanic black | 0.621 | 0.826 |
| | (−1.21) | (−0.49) |
|   Non-Hispanic other | 0.756 | 0.631 |
| | (−0.44) | (−0.81) |
|   Hispanic | 1.033 | 1.230 |
| | (0.10) | (0.61) |
| Age (in years) | 1.013 | 1.008 |
| | (1.60) | (0.95) |
| Educational attainment | | |
|   Less than a college degree | 1 | 1 |
|   College degree or higher | 2.072*** | 1.839** |
| | (3.31) | (2.73) |
| Income (in $1,000s) | 1.002 | 1.002 |
| | (1.02) | (0.86) |
| Rural/urban residence | | |
|   Urban | 1 | 1 |
|   Rural | 1.174 | 1.208 |
| | (0.62) | (0.70) |

## Table C.3—Continued

| Variable | Regression Model 1: Positive Impression | Regression Model 2: Positive Impression[a] |
|---|---|---|
| Marital status | | |
| Not married | 1 | 1 |
| Married | 1.200 | 1.188 |
| | (0.82) | (0.76) |
| Election participation | | |
| Voted in 2016 | 1 | 1 |
| Did not vote in 2016 | 0.428** | 0.483* |
| | (−2.65) | (−2.31) |
| Political conservatism | 0.954 | 1.018 |
| | (−0.41) | (0.16) |
| Knowledge of Foreign Service | — | 1.472*** |
| | — | (6.54) |
| Observations | 1,762 | 1,762 |

NOTES: Results are shown in odds ratios with $t$ statistics in parentheses.
[a] Regression model 2 includes controls on knowledge of foreign service.
* $p < 0.05$, ** $p < 0.01$, *** $p < 0.001$.

**TABLE C.4**

**Results of Ordinary Least Squares Regression for Sum of Number of Functions Performed by Diplomats Known by Respondents, 2020**

| Variable | |
|---|---|
| Gender | |
|     Female | 0 |
|     Male | 0.533* |
| | (2.30) |
| Race/ethnicity | |
|     Non-Hispanic white | 0 |
|     Non-Hispanic black | −1.187* |
| | (−2.56) |
|     Non-Hispanic other | 0.354 |
| | (0.84) |
|     Hispanic | −0.779* |
| | (−2.13) |
| Age (in years) | 0.017* |
| | (2.07) |
| Educational attainment | |
|     Less than a college degree | 0 |
|     College degree or higher | 0.495* |
| | (2.42) |
| Income (in $1,000s) | 0.001 |
| | (0.21) |
| Rural/urban residence | |
|     Urban | 0 |
|     Rural | −0.115 |
| | (−0.39) |
| Marital status | |
|     Not married | 0 |
|     Married | −0.038 |
| | (−0.12) |

## Table C.4—Continued

| Variable | |
|---|---|
| Election participation | |
| Voted in 2016 | 0 |
| Did not vote in 2016 | −0.640* |
| | (−2.06) |
| Political conservatism | −0.181 |
| | (−1.72) |
| Observations | 1,762 |

NOTES: Results shown are linear regression coefficients with $t$ statistics in parentheses.

* $p < 0.05$, ** $p < 0.01$, *** $p < 0.001$.

## TABLE C.5
## Results of Logistic Regressions for Perceptions of American Diplomats as Trustworthy or Politically Biased, 2020

| Variable | (1) Trustworthy | (2) Politically Biased |
|---|---|---|
| Gender | | |
|   Female | 1 | 1 |
|   Male | 1.297 | 1.182 |
| | (1.14) | (0.79) |
| Race/ethnicity | | |
|   Non-Hispanic white | 1 | 1 |
|   Non-Hispanic black | 0.628 | 1.504 |
| | (−1.29) | (1.12) |
|   Non-Hispanic other | 0.519 | 1.198 |
| | (−1.30) | (0.37) |
|   Hispanic | 1.447 | 1.327 |
| | (1.08) | (0.87) |
| Age (in years) | 1.010 | 0.999 |
| | (1.19) | (−0.14) |
| Educational attainment | | |
|   Less than a college degree | 1 | 1 |
|   College degree or higher | 2.092*** | 1.143 |
| | (3.23) | (0.61) |
| Income (in $1,000s) | 1.006** | 1.004 |
| | (2.98) | (1.72) |
| Rural/urban residence | | |
|   Urban | 1 | 1 |
|   Rural | 0.962 | 1.070 |
| | (−0.16) | (0.30) |
| Marital status | | |
|   Not married | 1 | 1 |
|   Married | 1.524 | 1.235 |
| | (1.65) | (0.92) |

## Table C.5—Continued

| Variable | (1) Trustworthy | (2) Politically Biased |
|---|---|---|
| Election participation | | |
| Voted in 2016 | 1 | 1 |
| Did not vote in 2016 | 0.710 | 1.090 |
| | (−1.18) | (0.30) |
| Political conservatism | 1.050 | 1.173 |
| | (0.49) | (1.61) |
| Knowledge of Foreign Service | 1.216* | 1.233*** |
| | (2.24) | (3.62) |
| Observations | 1,762 | 1,761 |

NOTES: Results are shown in odds ratios with $t$ statistics in parentheses.
* $p < 0.05$, ** $p < 0.01$, *** $p < 0.001$.

**TABLE C.6**
**Results of Ordinary Least Squares Regression for Sum of Number of Roles That Career Ambassadors Were Considered More Effective at Than Appointed Ambassadors, 2021**

| Variable | |
|---|---|
| Gender | |
|     Female | 0 |
|     Male | 0.352* |
| | (2.18) |
| Race/ethnicity | |
|     Non-Hispanic white | 0 |
|     Non-Hispanic black | −0.599* |
| | (−2.45) |
|     Non-Hispanic other | −0.378 |
| | (−1.06) |
|     Hispanic | −0.547* |
| | (−2.38) |
| Age (in years) | 0.003 |
| | (0.49) |
| Educational attainment | |
|     Less than a college degree | 0 |
|     College degree or higher | 0.412* |
| | (2.44) |
| Income (in $1,000s) | 0.004* |
| | (2.55) |
| Rural/urban residence | |
|     Urban | 0 |
|     Rural | −0.151 |
| | (−0.88) |
| Marital status | |
|     Not married | 0 |
|     Married | −0.084 |
| | (−0.51) |

## Table C.6—Continued

| Variable | |
|---|---|
| Election participation | |
|     Voted in 2016 | 0 |
|     Did not vote in 2016 | −0.199 |
| | (−0.91) |
| Political conservatism | −0.131 |
| | (−1.67) |
| Knowledge of Foreign Service | 0.111** |
| | (2.80) |
| Observations | 1,754 |

NOTES: Results shown are linear regression coefficients with $t$ statistics in parentheses.

* $p < 0.05$, ** $p < 0.01$, *** $p < 0.001$.

## TABLE C.7
## Results of Logistic Regressions for Perceptions of American Diplomats as Trustworthy or Politically Biased, Controlling for Geographic Region, 2020 and 2021

|  | (1) 2020 | (2) 2021 |
|---|---|---|
| Region |  |  |
|   Northeast | 0.450** | 0.336*** |
|  | (−2.75) | (−3.27) |
|   Midwest | 0.495* | 1 |
|  | (−2.18) |  |
|   South | 0.833 | 0.886 |
|  | (−0.71) | (−0.41) |
|   West | 1 | 0.601 |
|  |  | (−1.66) |
| Gender |  |  |
|   Female | 1 | 1 |
|   Male | 1.439 | 2.019*** |
|  | (1.78) | (3.50) |
| Race/ethnicity |  |  |
|   Non-Hispanic white | 1 | 1 |
|   Non-Hispanic black | 0.810 | 0.519 |
|  | (−0.54) | (−1.67) |
|   Non-Hispanic other | 0.507 | 0.349 |
|  | (−1.26) | (−1.93)) |
|   Hispanic | 1.079 | 0.880 |
|  | (0.23) | (−0.37) |
| Age (in years) | 1.006 | 1.009 |
|  | (0.77) | (1.26) |
| Educational attainment |  |  |
|   Less than a college degree | 1 | 1 |
|   College degree or higher | 1.837** | 2.035*** |
|  | (2.69) | (3.31) |

## Table C.7—Continued

|  | (1) 2020 | (2) 2021 |
|---|---|---|
| Income (in $1,000s) | 1.002 | 1.005* |
|  | (0.92) | (2.40) |
| Rural/urban residence |  |  |
| Urban | 1 | 1 |
| Rural | 1.224 | 1.089 |
|  | (0.74) | (0.33) |
| Marital status |  |  |
| Not married | 1 | 1 |
| Married | 1.147 | 0.904 |
|  | (0.61) | (−0.45) |
| Election participation |  |  |
| Voted in 2016 | 1 | 1 |
| Did not vote in 2016 | 0.522* | 0.617 |
|  | (−2.12) | (−1.68) |
| Political conservatism | 1.005 | 0.823 |
|  | (0.05) | (−1.77) |
| Knowledge of Foreign Service | 1.479*** | 1.277*** |
|  | (6.59) | (4.52) |
| Observations | 1,761 | 1,761 |

NOTES: Results are shown in odds ratios with $t$ statistics in parentheses.
* $p < 0.05$, ** $p < 0.01$, *** $p < 0.001$.

APPENDIX D

# Focus Group Protocol

AS PARTICIPANTS (SIGN ON TO/ENTER) THE MEETING THEY WILL BE REMINDED TO:
- TURN OFF CELL PHONES
- FOR TEAM PARTICIPANTS: MOVE TO A PRIVATE AREA

I.  **Introduction** (5 minutes)

Hello. My name is (NAME) and I work at RAND, a nonprofit research center based in Santa Monica, California. *[INTRODUCE ANY OTHER PEOPLE IN ROOM OR OBSERVERS: e.g., "Joining me today is (insert)."]*

Our discussion today is part of a larger project that is funded by the Cox Foundation.

We are part of a research team that is trying to learn more about what people know about the U.S. Foreign Service.

We really appreciate that you agreed to talk with us today.

You were invited today because we want to talk with people around the country about what they know about the Foreign Service, about what our diplomats do, and any thoughts about how the Foreign Service works.

But don't worry, you don't need to be familiar with any of these topics to participate in today's discussion.

As you know, we are videotaping this focus group.

The purpose of the video is to make sure we have a complete and accurate record of what we talk about.

We plan to transcribe the video and use it to write up a report of what we learn.

Once the transcription is made, we will destroy the video.

Our report will include quotes, but no one's name will appear in the report, and we will not include any information that would let a reader know who you are.

We are taking all possible measures to protect your confidentiality and privacy.

So, please use only your own and other's first names during the group.

Here are some other things to keep in mind for our discussion:

- There are no right or wrong answers, but there are different points of view. Please feel free to share your point of view and experience, even if it differs from what others have said. We are interested in both positive and negative comments.

- If you don't want to answer a particular question or discuss a particular topic, just say so—you don't have to answer or discuss anything you don't want to.
- We want to hear from as many of you as possible, so please give everyone on the call opportunities to participate. It is best if only one person speaks at a time.
- Especially because we are recording, please speak up (and also please do not have side conversations).
- We do have a limited time, and several issues to discuss. Please don't be offended if I ever have to interrupt a conversation so that we can move on.
- We also ask that each of you respect the privacy of everyone in the room and not share or repeat what is said here. However, since someone in the group may decide to not follow these instructions, we recommend you avoid sharing anything that you don't want anyone to repeat outside the group. (Please also make sure you are in a private place and that no one else is able to hear the group.)
- Today's conversation will last about 90 minutes.
- As a reminder, you will each receive $100 for your participation today.

*(REMIND PARTICIPANTS TO TURN OFF CELL PHONES.)*
*NOTETAKERS: ALIGN WITH ASSIGNED NUMBERS, CLOCKWISE OR COUNTERCLOCKWISE.*

Thank you in advance for your time today; we really value your input. Do you have any questions before we get started? Let's get going then.

**II.     Warm Up** (10 minutes)
First, let's start by having everyone introduce themselves. Starting with (SPECIFY PERSON), please tell us your first name and one word that describes yourself.

**Section 1: Background Questions and Introductions** (10 minutes)

- How closely do you follow the news of developments around the world outside the U.S.?
    - Where do you get most of your news? (e.g., online news outlets, Facebook, Twitter, TV, print newspapers)

**Section 2: Overall Impressions of Diplomacy** (30 minutes)

- When you hear the phrase "American diplomacy," what kind of things come to mind?
- What do you think the goals of American diplomacy are?

We are interested in what people around the country know about the work of diplomats, and we hope to get a discussion going about what you think about it and why. I just want to emphasize again that there are no right or wrong answers, and your opinions are important to us. It is okay if you don't know anything about American diplomats and the work they do; that's also important for us to find out.

So, we've just put up a brief description of American diplomats and diplomacy.

DISPLAY ON SCREEN AND READ ALOUD:

*American Foreign Service Officers (FSOs) are also called diplomats. Diplomats generally work for the U.S. Department of State. The Department of State is the part of the federal government that is carrying out the nation's foreign policy and international relations. Diplomats represent U.S. policies to foreign governments and foreign citizens, negotiate and enforce agreements we have with other countries, protect American citizens when they are abroad, make decisions about whether to approve visas for foreigners to travel to the U.S., and lead other activities done at embassies abroad or in Washington aimed at advancing and securing American economic and security interests around the world.*

Let me start by asking you about your overall sense of American diplomacy. (Diplomacy is how countries interact, or how the U.S. deals with other countries.)

- What do you think about American diplomacy?
  - Is it generally successful/unsuccessful, or effective/ineffective?
  - Or do you not have enough information to make that judgment (form an opinion/it is OK to not have an opinion)?
- Why do you say that?
- Do you think that diplomacy abroad contributes to our national security?
- Why or why not?
- POSSIBLE PROMPTS:
  - No, our focus needs to be at home.
  - Yes, future threats and opportunities (e.g., climate, migration) are abroad.
  - Yes, we must defend our values and democracy abroad to preserve them at home.
  - No, America should not search for "monsters to destroy" (famous quote of President John Quincy Adams).
- How much do you think Americans pay attention to foreign policy and diplomacy?
  - Do you think Americans pay enough attention to foreign policy and diplomacy?

**Section 3: U.S. Embassies** (30 minutes)

As you (may) know, the United States, like most countries, has 307 embassies, consulates, and missions all over the world.

What do you think are the most important things U.S. embassies overseas do?
- Why do you think this?

On the screen, there is a list of some things that U.S. embassies do.

[READ ALOUD AND DISPLAY ON SCREEN]

- Protecting American citizens in trouble
- Representing U.S. policy to foreign governments and publics
- Promoting American exports from U.S. farms and manufacturers
- Deciding on visa applications from foreigners seeking to visit the U.S.
- Reporting on developments in foreign countries
- Promote/explain U.S. values
- Engage foreign publics to inform and influence them about U.S. values and policy priorities to enhance U.S.'s international image or generate a more favorable view of the United States abroad
- Informing U.S. foreign policy by providing actionable feedback to National Security Council/the executive branch

Did you know that U.S. embassies and diplomats did all of these things?
- What was a surprise to you?
- Which of these activities do you think is the most/least important? Why?

**Section 4: General Thoughts About Diplomats** (20 minutes)
We just talked about what diplomats do. American diplomats staff our embassies, consulates, and missions all over the world, some of them in remote and dangerous cities. In war zones, American diplomats serve alongside the U.S. military.

- What is your view of American diplomats—is it generally positive or negative? (Do you even have a view of diplomats?)
- Have you ever had any interaction with a U.S. diplomat (or anyone in the Foreign Service)? (Can you tell us a bit about it?)
- Do you think we should have diplomats stationed abroad?
  - Why/why not?
- What is it, if anything, that civilian engagement through diplomacy adds to the protection of US national interests abroad?
- POSSIBLE PROMPTS:
  - Do you think a better understanding of, or appreciation for, U.S. interests that our diplomats provide, enhances our national security, or advances our national interests? Why or why not? How so?
- Do you have any concerns about diplomats (or for the diplomats that are stationed abroad)? Why?
- POSSIBLE PROMPTS:
  - Safety concerns, national loyalty, for example?
  - What happens to them in foreign conflict (e.g., Iran)?
  - Are they potential targets for terrorists (e.g., Benghazi)?
  - That they "go native" and are more sympathetic to foreign interests than our own.
  - Diplomats don't represent Americans.

What, if anything, do you think U.S. diplomats need to do their job better? How do you think U.S. diplomats (or the Department of State) can improve their efficiency/effectiveness in carrying out their role?

- American diplomats focus predominantly on their responsibilities in Washington, D.C., and in foreign countries. Do you think there is value in American diplomats spending time in American communities around the country? Why?
- (IF SO) How should there be greater interaction with our diplomats?
- POSSIBLE PROMPTS:
    - Through city (local) governments
    - Through universities
    - Through civic organizations (e.g., clubs, etc.)
    - Through social media
    - Through Department of State–funded or private/citizen-run organizations (e.g., International Visitor Leadership Program)

**Section 5: Choosing Diplomats** (20 minutes)
American diplomats are chosen through competitive written and oral exams that test their global knowledge and judgment. Candidates are also assessed on their knowledge of foreign languages, though knowing a foreign language is not a requirement to become a diplomat.

- What do you think are the most important criteria for choosing America's diplomats?
- What should they know, or be able to do, or what kinds of personal qualities are important? Why?

On the screen, there is a list of possible criteria for choosing diplomats. Let's look at each one.
[READ ALOUD AND DISPLAY ON SCREEN]

- Language fluency
- Understanding global affairs
- Bravery in the face of danger
- Negotiating skill
- Public speaking
- Diversity

Are there any other criteria that you think should be considered?

Which of the criteria do you think is the most important? What about the least important?

**Section 6: The Future of Diplomacy** (15 minutes)

- How important do you think diplomacy will be in the future? Do globalization or technology make it potentially more or less important, for example?
- (Possible prompts)
    - Very, because the world is ever more connected
    - Not so much: U.S. is too involved abroad; need to pull back, let foreigners solve own problems
    - Not so much, technology connects us otherwise, don't need people on the ground
    - Very, to contain security threats and disease before they come to our shores
- Should diplomats or the military lead efforts in most countries abroad?
    - Why, or why not?
- Thinking about all of the parts of the government and the military, what parts of our government should be the most important in the making of American foreign policy?
- PROBE: What about . . .
- The White House
- The State Department
- The Pentagon
- The Congress
- The Treasury
- Or something else?

- In the future, do you think the U.S. should spend more to protect our interests in the world, about the same, or less? Why?

Any other comments/reflections?

REMIND ABOUT PROJECT DESCRIPTION, THANK AND END

# Abbreviations

| | |
|---|---|
| ALP | American Life Panel |
| ANES | American National Election Studies |
| CCGA | Chicago Council on Global Affairs |
| FSO | Foreign Service Officer |
| ISIS | the Islamic State of Iraq and Syria |
| NSRD | National Security Research Division |

# References

Aldrich, John H., Christopher Gelpi, Peter Feaver, Jason Reifler, and Kristin Thompson Sharp, "Foreign Policy and the Electoral Connection," *Annual Review of Political Science*, Vol. 9, 2006, pp. 477–502.

American National Election Studies, homepage, undated. As of January 10, 2022:
https://electionstudies.org/

ANES—*See* American National Election Studies.

Baum, Matthew A., and Tim Groeling, "Shot by the Messenger: Partisan Cues and Public Opinion Regarding National Security and War," *Political Behavior*, Vol. 31, No. 2, June 2009, pp. 157–186.

Baum, Matthew A., and Philip B. K. Potter, "Media, Public Opinion, and Foreign Policy in the Age of Social Media," *Journal of Politics*, Vol. 81, No. 2, 2019, pp. 747–756.

Berinsky, Adam J., *Silent Voices: Opinion Polls and Political Participation in America*, Princeton, N.J.: Princeton University Press, 2004.

Bouton, Marshall M., Rachel Bronson, Gregory Holyk, Catherine Hug, Steven Kull, Benjamin I. Page, Silvia Veltcheva, and Thomas Wright, *Global Views 2010: Constrained Internationalism—Adapting to New Realities. Results of a 2010 National Survey of American Public Opinion*, Chicago, Ill.: Chicago Council on Global Affairs, September 16, 2010. As of January 10, 2022:
https://www.thechicagocouncil.org/research/public-opinion-survey/2010-chicago-council-survey

Bouton, Marshall M., Catherine Hug, Steven Kull, Mike Kulma, Benjamin I. Page, Teresita C. Schaffer, Silvia Veltcheva, Christopher B. Whitney, and Dali L. Yang, *Global Views 2006: The United States and the Rise of China and India—Results of a 2006 Multination Survey of Public Opinion*, Chicago, Ill.: Chicago Council on Global Affairs and the Asia Society, October 11, 2006. As of January 10, 2022:
https://www.thechicagocouncil.org/research/public-opinion-survey/2006-chicago-council-survey

Bouton, Marshall M., and Benjamin I. Pahe, *Worldviews 2002: American Public Opinion & Foreign Policy*, Chicago, Ill.: Chicago Council on Global Affairs, October 1, 2002. As of January 10, 2022:
https://www.thechicagocouncil.org/research/public-opinion-survey/2002-chicago-council-survey

Budiman, Abby, "Americans Are More Positive About the Long-Term Rise in U.S. Racial and Ethnic Diversity Than in 2016," Washington, D.C.: Pew Research Center, October 1, 2020. As of January 23, 2022:
https://www.pewresearch.org/fact-tank/2020/10/01/americans-are-more-positive-about-the-long-term-rise-in-u-s-racial-and-ethnic-diversity-than-in-2016/

Burns, Nicholas, Marc Grossman, and Marcie Ries, *American Diplomacy Project: A U.S. Diplomatic Service for the 21st Century*, Cambridge, Mass.: Belfer Center for Science and International Affairs, Harvard Kennedy School, November 2020. As of November 15, 2020:
https://www.belfercenter.org/sites/default/files/2020-11/DiplomaticService.pdf

Caudill, Shannon W., Andrew M. Leonard, and Richard D. Thresher, "Interagency Leadership: The Case for Strengthening the Department of State," *American Diplomacy*, April 2008.

Cavari, Amnon, and Guy Freedman, "Partisan Cues and Opinion Formation on Foreign Policy," *American Politics Research*, Vol. 47, No. 1, 2019, pp. 29–57.

Delli Carpini, Michael X., and Scott Keeter, *What Americans Know About Politics and Why It Matters*, New Haven, Conn.: Yale University Press, 1996.

Delli Carpini, Michael X., Scott Keeter, and Sharon Webb, "The Impact of Presidential Debates," in Pippa Norris, ed., *Politics and the Press: The News Media and Their Influences*, Boulder, Colo.: Rienner, 1997, pp. 145–164.

*The Economist*, "The Dereliction of American Diplomacy," August 15, 2020. As of December 27, 2020:
https://www.economist.com/international/2020/08/11/how-much-does-americas-missing-diplomatic-leadership-matter

Frankovic, Kathy, "Only One-Third of Americans Have a Valid U.S. Passport," YouGov, April 21, 2021. As of March 15, 2022:
https://today.yougov.com/topics/travel/articles-reports/2021/04/21/only-one-third-americans-have-valid-us-passport

Hannah, Mark, and Caroline Gray, *Diplomacy & Restraint: The Worldview of American Voters*, New York: Eurasia Group Foundation, September 2020. As of March 15, 2022:
https://egfound.org/wp-content/uploads/2020/09/EGF_Diplomacy_And_Restraint_The_Worldview_of_American_Voters_September2020.pdf

Holsti, Ole R., *Public Opinion and American Foreign Policy*, revised edition, Ann Arbor, Mich.: University of Michigan Press, 2004.

Holsti, Ole R., and James N. Rosenau, *American Leadership in World Affairs: Vietnam and the Breakdown of Consensus*, Boston: Allen & Unwin, 1984.

House Foreign Affairs Committee, "Meeks Introduces Legislative Package to Renew American Leadership Abroad in Face of China Challenge," press release, Washington, D.C., May 25, 2021. As of March 15, 2022:
https://foreignaffairs.house.gov/2021/5/meeks-introduces-legislative-package-to-renew-american-leadership-abroad-in-face-of-china-challenge

Hudson, John, "U.S. Repeals Propaganda Ban, Spreads Government-Made News to Americans," *Foreign Policy*, July 14, 2013. As of March 15, 2022:
https://foreignpolicy.com/2013/07/14/u-s-repeals-propaganda-ban-spreads-government-made-news-to-americans/

Johns, Robert, "Tracing Foreign Policy Decisions: A Study of Citizens' Use of Heuristics," *British Journal of Politics and International Relations*, Vol. 11, No. 4, 2009, pp. 574–592.

Lenz, Gabriel S., "Learning and Opinion Change, Not Priming: Reconsidering the Priming Hypothesis," *American Journal of Political Science*, Vol. 53, No. 4, October 2009, pp. 821–837.

Mordecai, Mara, and Moira Fagan, "How U.S. Views on Foreign Policy and International Cooperation Are Linked," Washington, D.C.: Pew Research Center, May 5, 2021. As of November 4, 2021:
https://www.pewresearch.org/fact-tank/2021/04/23/americans-views-of-key-foreign-policy-goals-depend-on-their-attitudes-toward-international-cooperation/

Morello, Carol, "Pompeo Accused of Mixing Politics and Diplomacy as Election Nears," *Washington Post*, October 5, 2020.

National Defense Authorization Act for 2013, H.R. 4310, Section 1078, December 28, 2021. As of March 15, 2022:
https://www.govtrack.us/congress/bills/112/hr4310/text

Ostrom, Charles W., and Brian L. Job, "The President and the Political Use of Force," *American Political Science Review*, Vol. 80, No. 2, 1986, pp. 541–566.

Pew Research Center, "Question 34: USPSRA.042601.R12G," *Pew Research Center Poll: April 2001, News Interest Index*, 2001. As of May 11, 2022:
https://doi.org/10.25940/ROPER-31095742

Pew Research Center, "Question 10: USPSRA.070909A.R02IF2," *Pew Research Center Poll: June 2009, Science Knowledge Omnibus Survey*, 2009. As of May 11, 2022:
https://doi.org/10.25940/ROPER-31095961

Pew Research Center, "Question 53: USPSRA.022213.R28FF1," *Pew Research Center Poll: February 2013 Political Survey*, 2013. As of May 11, 2022:
https://doi.org/10.25940/ROPER-31096190

Pew Research Center, "Question 65: USPSRA.042417.R41DF1," *Pew Research Center: April 2017 Political Survey*, 2017. As of May 11, 2022:
https://doi.org/10.25940/ROPER-31114967

Pew Research Center, "6. Views of Foreign Policy," webpage, December 17, 2019. As of December 27, 2020:
https://www.pewresearch.org/politics/2019/12/17/6-views-of-foreign-policy/

Pew Research Center, "Majority of Americans Confident in Biden's Handling of Foreign Policy as Term Begins," webpage, February 2021. As of January 10, 2022:
https://www.pewresearch.org/politics/2021/02/24/majority-of-americans-confident-in-bidens-handling-of-foreign-policy-as-term-begins/

Pollard, Michael S., and Matthew D. Baird, *The RAND American Life Panel: Technical Description*, Santa Monica, Calif.: RAND Corporation, RR-1651, 2017. As of March 10, 2022:
https://www.rand.org/pubs/research_reports/RR1651.html

Pollard, Michael S., and Joshua Mendelsohn, *Methodology of the 2016 RAND Presidential Election Panel Survey (PEPS)*, Santa Monica, Calif.: RAND Corporation, RR-1460-RC/UCLA, 2016. As of March 11, 2022:
https://www.rand.org/pubs/research_reports/RR1460.html

RAND American Life Panel, homepage, 2020. As of March 15, 2022:
https://alpdata.rand.org/

Rielly, John E., ed., *American Public Opinion and U.S. Foreign Policy 1975*, Chicago, Ill.: Chicago Council on Foreign Relations, 1975. As of January 10, 2022:
https://www.thechicagocouncil.org/research/public-opinion-survey/1974-chicago-council-survey

Rielly, John E., ed., *American Public Opinion and U.S. Foreign Policy 1979*, Chicago, Ill.: Chicago Council on Foreign Relations, 1979. As of January 10, 2022:
https://www.thechicagocouncil.org/research/public-opinion-survey/1978-chicago-council-survey

Rielly, John E., ed., *American Public Opinion and U.S. Foreign Policy 1983*, Chicago, Ill.: Chicago Council on Foreign Relations, 1983. As of January 10, 2022:
https://www.thechicagocouncil.org/research/public-opinion-survey/1982-chicago-council-survey

Seligman, Lara, Andrew Desiderio, and Nahal Toosi, "State IG Launches Investigations into End of Afghanistan Operations," *Politico*, October 18, 2021. As of January 23, 2022:
https://www.politico.com/news/2021/10/18/
state-ig-investigations-afghanistan-operations-516207

Smeltz, Dina, Ivo Daalder, Karl Friedhoff, and Craig Kafura, *America Divided: Political Partisanship and U.S. Foreign Policy: Results of the 2015 Chicago Council Survey of American Public Opinion and U.S. Foreign Policy*, Chicago, Ill.: Chicago Council on Global Affairs, 2015.

Smeltz, Dina, Ivo Daalder, Karl Friedhoff, and Craig Kafura, *Results of the 2017 Chicago Council Survey of American Public Opinion and U.S. Foreign Policy: What Americans Think About America First*, Chicago, Ill.: Chicago Council on Global Affairs, 2017. As of March 15, 2022:
https://www.thechicagocouncil.org/research/
public-opinion-survey/2017-chicago-council-survey

Smeltz, Dina, Ivo Daalder, and Craig Kafura, *Foreign Policy in the Age of Retrenchment: Results of the 2014 Chicago Council Survey of American Public Opinion and U.S. Foreign Policy*, Chicago, Ill.: Chicago Council on Global Affairs, 2014. As of January 20, 2022:
https://www.thechicagocouncil.org/research/
public-opinion-survey/2014-chicago-council-survey

Smeltz, Dina, Ivo Daalder, Karl Friedhoff, Craig Kafura, and Brendan Helm, *Divided We Stand: Democrats and Republicans Diverge on U.S. Foreign Policy, Results of the 2020 Chicago Council Survey of American Public Opinion and U.S. Foreign Policy*, Chicago, Ill.: Lester Crown Center on U.S. Foreign Policy and Chicago Council on Global Affairs, 2020.

Smeltz, Dina, Ivo Daalder, Karl Friedhoff, Craig Kafura, and Emily Sullivan, *A Foreign Policy for the Middle Class—What Americans Think: Results of the 2021 Chicago Council Survey of American Public Opinion and U.S. Foreign Policy*, Chicago, Ill.: Lester Crown Center on U.S. Foreign Policy and Chicago Council on Global Affairs, 2021.

Smeltz, Dina, Ivo Daalder, Karl Friedhoff, Craig Kafura, and Lily Wojtowicz, *2018 Chicago Council Survey—America Engaged: American Public Opinion and U.S. Foreign Policy*, Chicago, Ill.: Lester Crown Center on U.S. Foreign Policy and Chicago Council on Global Affairs, 2018.

Smith, Jackie, Marina Karides, Marc Becker, Dorval Brunelle, Christopher Chase-Dunn, and Donatella Della Porta, *Global Democracy and the World Social Forums*, 2nd ed., Abingdon, UK: Routledge, 2014.

Smith, Tom W., Michael Davern, Jeremy Freese, and Stephen L. Morgan, "General Social Survey, 2006," machine-readable data file, Chicago, Ill.: NORC, 2019.

U.S. Code, Title 22, United States Information and Educational Exchange Act of 1948 (Smith-Mundt Act), Section 1431, Congressional Declaration of Objectives, 1948. As of March 15, 2022:
https://uscode.house.gov/view.xhtml?path=/prelim@title22/chapter18&edition=prelim

U.S. Department of State, "International Affairs Budgets," webpage, undated. As of March 15, 2022:
https://www.state.gov/plans-performance-budget/international-affairs-budgets/

U.S. Department of State, "Transformational Diplomacy," speech by Condoleezza Rice, Georgetown University, Washington, D.C., January 18, 2006. As of January 20, 2022:
https://2001-2009.state.gov/secretary/rm/2006/59306.htm

U.S. Department of State, "Remarks of Secretary of State Antony Blinken at the appointment of Ambassador Gina Abercrombie-Winstanley as Chief Diversity and Inclusion Officer," press release, April 12, 2021a. As of January 19, 2022:
https://www.state.gov/secretary-antony-j-blinken-at-the-announcement-of-ambassador-gina-abercrombie-winstanley-as-chief-diversity-and-inclusion-officer/

U.S. Department of State, "Secretary Antony J. Blinken on the Modernization of American Diplomacy," press release, October 27, 2021b. As of October 28, 2021:
https://www.state.gov/secretary-antony-j-blinken-on-the-modernization-of-american-diplomacy/